# Why It's OK
## to Be of Two Minds

Most of us experience the world through competing perspectives. A job or a religion seems important and fulfilling when looked at in one way, but from a different angle it seems tedious or ridiculous. A friend is obtuse from one point of view, wise from another. Continuing to hold both views at once can be unsettling, highlighting conflicts between our own judgments and values and undermining our ability to live purposefully and effectively.

Yet, as Jennifer Church argues in this book, inner conflict can be a good thing, and not just as a temporary road bump on the road to resolution. This book describes several desirable types of "double consciousness" – or being of two minds – and explains why and how they should be maintained. Church looks critically at some common ideas about identity, including a popular belief about narratives that suggests our lives should "make sense" as a story. She also examines how empathy can helpfully cause us to be of two minds, and how various forms of irony and laughter enable us to benefit from holding onto opposing views. Finally, Church [...]erit of acknowledging realit[...] l by fantasy.

*Why It's OK to Be of Two* [...]wo opposing views simultane[...] ne.

**Key Features**

- Argues against a long-standing philosophical idea: that it is important to resolve inner conflicts that result from competing systems of beliefs.
- Examines the role of empathy and friendship in maintaining a valuable form of double consciousness.
- Considers how irony and laughter allow us to dedicate ourselves to our particular projects while acknowledging their ultimate insignificance.
- Shows how fantasies that conflict with our beliefs can make a positive contribution to the way we live our lives.

**Jennifer Church** is a Professor of Philosophy at Vassar College in Poughkeepsie, New York. Her research addresses various topics in the philosophy of mind. She is the author of *Possibilities of Perception* (Oxford UP, 2013) and numerous articles on mental divisions and mental health.

## Why It's OK: The Ethics and Aesthetics of How We Live

Philosophers often build cogent arguments for unpopular positions. Recent examples include cases against marriage and pregnancy, for treating animals as our equals, and dismissing some popular art as aesthetically inferior. What philosophers have done less often is to offer compelling arguments for widespread and established human behavior, like getting married, having children, eating animals, and going to the movies. But if one role for philosophy is to help us reflect on our lives and build sound justifications for our beliefs and actions, it seems odd that philosophers would neglect arguments for the lifestyles most people – including many philosophers – actually lead. Unfortunately, philosophers' inattention to normalcy has meant that the ways of life that define our modern societies have gone largely without defense, even as whole literatures have emerged to condemn them.

**Why It's OK: The Ethics and Aesthetics of How We Live** seeks to remedy that. It's a series of books that provides accessible, sound, and often new and creative arguments for widespread ethical and aesthetic values. Made up of short volumes that assume no previous knowledge of philosophy from the reader, the series recognizes that philosophy is just as important for understanding what we already believe as it is for criticizing the status quo. The series isn't meant to make us complacent about what we value; rather, it helps and challenges us to think more deeply about the values that give our daily lives meaning.

Titles in Series:

**Why It's OK to Want to Be Rich**

Jason Brennan

**Why It's OK to Be of Two Minds**

Jennifer Church

**Why It's OK to Ignore Politics**

Christopher Freiman

**Why It's OK to Make Bad Choices**

William Glod

Selected Forthcoming Titles:

**Why It's OK to Get Married**

Christie J. Hartley

**Why It's OK to Love Bad Movies**

Matthew Strohl

**Why It's OK to Eat Meat**

Dan C. Shahar

**Why It's OK to Mind Your Own Business**

Justin Tosi and Brandon Warmke

**Why It's OK to Be Fat**

Rekha Nath

**Why It's OK to Be a Moral Failure**

Robert Talisse

**Why It's OK to Have Bad Grammar and Spelling**

Jessica Flanigan

For further information about this series, please visit: www.routledge.com/Why-Its-OK/book-series/WIOK

**Why It's OK** to Be of Two Minds

JENNIFER CHURCH

# Why It's OK
## to Be of Two Minds

Routledge
Taylor & Francis Group

NEW YORK AND LONDON

First published 2021
by Routledge
52 Vanderbilt Avenue, New York, NY 10017

and by Routledge
2 Park Square, Milton Park, Abingdon, Oxon, OX14 4RN

*Routledge is an imprint of the Taylor & Francis Group, an informa business*

*Library of Congress Cataloging-in-Publication Data*
A catalog record for this book has been requested

ISBN: 978-0-367-89863-2 (hbk)
ISBN: 978-0-367-89862-5 (pbk)
ISBN: 978-1-003-02154-4 (ebk)

Typeset in Joanna MT Pro and DIN pro
by Apex CoVantage, LLC

# Contents

*start ↗ 1/30/24*

We live in a time where most people belong to more than one culture, where most people undergo significant changes in outlook as they age, where most of us try to empathize with people from very different backgrounds than our own, and where most of us experience a significant disparity between the world we move in and the worlds we imagine. All of these dichotomies mean that we frequently find ourselves in states of "double consciousness" that give rise to various sorts of inner conflict. Inner conflict, like outer conflict, creates discomfort that we tend to avoid – by steering clear of whatever prompts the conflict, by discounting one or the other side of the conflict, or by seeking a harmonious resolution. However, these strategies are often unsuccessful or damaging. We are left with a lingering desire for inner coherence yet we doubt its feasibility. We attempt, by various means, to overcome the tension created by states of double consciousness but we do so without confidence in the task and without surprise at our failures.

Philosophy usually argues for coherent outlooks and whole selves. Wholeheartedness is valued because it makes us feel better and because a confident, undistracted actor is more likely to succeed. Also, we assume that the world itself is coherent, so true beliefs about that world must themselves be coherent.

Rejecting the ideal of wholeness seems to threaten the very idea of an objective world and the very possibility of a responsible self. These are not things that should be abandoned lightly. Thus, it is important to show how double consciousness can be embraced without losing our appreciation of individual selves inhabiting a common world. Double consciousness can be a creative, enlivening part of our lives. Explaining that is the task of this book.

Our perceptions, judgments, and values rely on relatively stable "schemas", or frameworks, for organizing the information received through our senses. These schemas draw on a mix of memories and expectations, background beliefs and desires, ongoing hopes and fears – all of which are themselves shaped by a mix of personal preferences, social encounters, and languages. The perspective from which a religious ceremony seems oppressive conflicts with the perspective from which it seems inspiring, and neither perspective relies on just one belief, one desire, or one memory. Likewise, there is usually an array of beliefs and desires underlying the view that a person is accomplished and quite a different array behind the view that they are manipulative. Given the plethora of worldviews that most people are exposed to, it is not surprising that most of us have adopted a variety of frameworks for organizing our experience, that these frameworks sometimes conflict with each other, and that more than one of them can be in play at the same time.

In extreme cases, the presence of conflicting points of view can result in the development of conflicting personalities, each of which competes for control of one's body – a dissociative disorder (or multiple personality syndrome). For those cases, it may be appropriate to speak of two selves within a single body. Similarly, there are cases in which one's conscious beliefs and desires conflict with one's unconscious beliefs and desires (in cases of self-deception, for example, or in cases where someone is unconsciously ashamed of something that she consciously accepts).[1] In the everyday cases I will be concerned with, however, the contrasting points of view exist as parts of a single self who is quite aware of the conflict. (I say more about the nature of selves and consciousness in Chapter 1.)

People differ in their ability to remain of two minds, and some mindsets conflict more than others. We are bound to feel conflicted, though, if we hold onto one point of view that recommends a particular choice (a face-saving lie, or a lucrative profession, for example) and another point of view that condemns that choice; or if we adopt one conceptual schema that causes us to value creativity alongside another schema that causes us to value logical clarity. Life would be easier, certainly, if we were free of inner conflict. But there are some kinds of double consciousness that are worth preserving – not only because of the added richness they bring to our lives but also because of the added knowledge, the added flexibility, and the added empathy they provide.

The ideal of wholeness has been criticized from a number of directions. Advocates for diversity within a society can become advocates for diversity within individual members of that society – reasoning that if acceptance of conflicting perspectives is healthy for a society at large it can be healthy for an individual as well. Many people worry that attempts at unity (within a society or within a person) tend to silence or suppress certain voices, making a state of anarchy (both inner and outer) preferable to any attempt at coherence. Scholars of human behavior, moreover, have documented the advantages of approaching problems from more than one perspective and of engaging different parts of the brain at the same time. Most radical of all are various attacks on the very idea of a mind-independent world – a world that is the way it is regardless of how we think about it. If there is no such reality, then we are free to construct multiple and conflicting realities for ourselves. All of these criticisms of wholeness deserve to be considered but, as we shall see, some are more compelling than others. *aha*

\* \* \*

Chapter 1 clarifies what it means to be "of two minds". Various examples are considered, focusing on the experiences of people with a background in two different cultures: W.E.B. Du Bois's description of double consciousness among African-Americans, Ralph Waldo Emerson's attempts to combine spiritualism and reason, Adrian Piper's identity as both an artist and a philosopher, and several other examples from everyday life. Double consciousness is explained as a state in which we use contrasting schemas to organize our experience, where the contrasts create significant and lasting mental conflict. People who have been raised in two (or more) different cultures frequently experience double consciousness, as do people who belong to two or more different subcultures – which is most of us. I review various arguments for overcoming conflict *in general* and find them unconvincing. I then review some standard ways of overcoming inner conflict – through resolution, separation, and dissolution – and show why these are undesirable options *for the cases under consideration*. How best to deal with the inner conflict of double consciousness remains a question, however, and three different models for meeting this challenge are introduced: a juggler model, an isometrics model, and a disruptor model. (These three models provide guidance in subsequent chapters as well.)

Chapter 2 addresses a kind of double consciousness that results from keeping a past version of ourselves alive in memory. Insofar as we recall the perspective of that past self "from the inside", and insofar as that past perspective clashes with our present perspective, we experience significant mental conflict. Something similar occurs when we imagine our future selves. One way of dealing with this mental conflict is to embed both points of view in a narrative that runs from the past to the present and into the future. Another way of dealing with the conflict is to insist that "the past is past" and no longer a part of oneself. These options are criticized, and some better alternatives are suggested.

Chapter 3 considers cases where we carry another person's point of view "within" us. These include cases where we have internalized the point of view of a parent or a teacher, cases where we empathize with someone we know, and cases where we love or are in love. There are different ways in which we can go about imagining another person's point of view. Empathy, however, requires us to imagine another person's experience "from the inside" and that can create an inner conflict despite our knowledge that the other's outlook belongs to that other person. The juggler and isometrics models introduced at the end of Chapter 1 point to some promising ways of dealing with these conflicts.

Chapter 4 is concerned with cases where we are of two minds because we hold onto both a narrow and a wide view of some situation. From a narrow point of view, our particular activities and feelings – working hard to achieve our goals, indignation at an insult, fear of death – can seem extremely important, yet from a wider point of view they seem quite unimportant. Holding onto both points of view feels like an important part of being human, but the juxtaposition of these two perspectives creates an important sort of inner conflict. The double stance of irony has been a popular but problematic response. The pursuit of non-attachment is another. These responses, however, can make the juxtaposition of narrow and wider perspectives into a loss rather than a gain. Different varieties of laughter, and different varieties of surrealism, point to more enlivening ways of keeping narrow and wide perspectives in play together.

Chapter 5 explores a type of double consciousness that results from projecting a fantasy onto the reality of our situation without actually believing that fantasy – imagining that everything in the world is conscious, for example, or imagining that, eventually, virtue will be rewarded and evil will be punished. These are not simply cases of entertaining a fantasy alongside what we take to be true, nor are they cases of refusing to acknowledge what one knows to be true; they are framing techniques that enable us to live *as if* the world were one way while fully aware that it is some other way. Philosophers have discussed "as if" living with respect to scientific theories, with respect to the illusion of free will, and with respect to the imagined unity of persons. A close look at each of these cases suggests that only some of them have the features that justify the associated states of double consciousness.

This book is not a manifesto on behalf of inner conflict or dissociated minds. Many sorts of inner conflict should be overcome, and many types of dissociation are undesirable. Some cases of undesirable double consciousness are discussed in individual chapters. The closing Addendum gives a more general account of when it *not* okay to be of two minds. These include cases where one or the other of the competing schemas is seriously misleading about the nature of the world, cases where one or the other of the competing schemas is seriously damaging to ourselves or to others, and cases where retaining two schemas functions as a way to avoid being committed to either.

The five types of double consciousness defended in this book should be familiar to almost everyone; we all have been influenced by different cultures, we all have memories of past selves that were different from our present self, we all empathize with people that are important to us, we all look at things from both narrow and wide points of view, and we all rely on certain fantasies to direct our dealings with reality. Whereas much theorizing about these things seeks to eliminate the associated conflicts, I argue for the importance of preserving – and, in some cases, intensifying – the conflict. I try to show, moreover, how being of two minds, approached in the right way, can be both enlivening and enlightening.

*goal*

# One

We make out of the quarrel with others, rhetoric, but of the quarrel with ourselves, poetry.

(Yeats 25)

Yeats's remark is not just a claim about what motivates him, or anyone else, to write poetry. It is a claim about poetry's ability to grapple with inner conflicts by sustaining more than one perspective or more than one set of meanings at the same time.[1] The poems of Baudelaire, for example, have been described as "seeing two world pictures at the same time. . . . Like a faulty telescope, the two images do not merge into one: they remain simultaneous, each as if refuting the other" (Meltzer 13–14). States of double consciousness are not unique to poetry, of course; they can be found throughout our everyday lives.

## BACKGROUND

The term "double consciousness" is most familiar from the writing of W.E.B. Du Bois, who, in 1903, described the inner conflict experienced by "black folk" who have internalized the ideals and judgments of white America, on the one hand, while still embracing their "Negro" heritage, on the other.

It is a peculiar sensation, this double-consciousness, this sense of always looking at one's self through the eyes of others, of measuring one's soul by the tape of a world that looks on in amused contempt and pity. One ever feels his two-ness – an American, a Negro; two souls, two thoughts, two unreconciled strivings; two warring ideals in one dark body.

(Du Bois 3)

The double consciousness described by Du Bois is not a simple combination of other people's derogatory view of oneself, now internalized, alongside some retained sense of self-worth; Du Bois does not recommend a simple rejection of the oppressor's point of view. What he describes is, instead, a "war" between two sets of worthwhile ideals. He endorses the ideals of white America insofar as they promote "civilization, culture, righteousness and progress"; yet he recognizes how focusing on these values feeds the view that uneducated Negros are "ignorant" and "barbaric". Likewise, he praises the value of physical work, of "simple faith and reverence", and of "jovial good humor"; yet he recognizes how focusing on those values makes white America appear to be "a dusty desert of dollars and smartness", full of "cruel wit" and "dyspeptic blundering". Both perspectives may be valuable, but they are (so far) "unreconciled" insofar as each perspective casts the other in a negative light.

The double consciousness of "black folk" in America is, accordingly, both a burden and an opportunity. On the one hand, it is a source of stress, shame, mutually undermining impulses, and escapist strategies. "This waste of double aims, this seeking to satisfy two unreconciled ideals, has wrought sad havoc with the courage and faith and deeds of ten thousand

thousand people, – has sent them often wooing false gods and invoking false means of salvation, and at times has even seemed about to make them ashamed of themselves" (4). On the other hand, insofar as Negro Americans (unlike white Americans) feel the pull of both sets of ideals, Du Bois considers them well-positioned to advance humanity to a more inclusive greatness.

> In this merging he wishes neither of the older selves to be lost. He does not wish to Africanize America, for America has too much to teach the world and Africa. He wouldn't bleach his Negro blood in a flood of white Americanism, for he knows that Negro blood has a message for the world.
>
> (3)

> Work, culture, liberty, – all these we need, not singly but together, not successively but together, each growing and aiding each, and all striving toward that vaster ideal that swims before the Negro people, . . . in order that some day on American soil two world-races may give each to each those characteristics both so sadly lack.
>
> of ?
>
> (7)

(I discuss Du Bois's understanding of how such opposed ideals can be reconciled in a later section.)

Du Bois's description of the double consciousness of African-Americans has been widely adopted, modified, and extended by feminists, literary critics, and critical race theorists. Women, as another subjugated group, have been described as having a double consciousness insofar as they have internalized a male perspective while also retaining their own independent perspective on themselves and on the world. Authors have been read as expressing their own double consciousness regarding race, gender, and sexual orientation through characters that oscillate between conformity and rebellion, through stories that revolve around ghosts and doubles, and through words that invite contradictory interpretations.[2] And a growing appreciation of the complexity of race in relation to class, gender, sexual preference, religion, and nationality has led to talk of not just double consciousness but triple and quadruple consciousness insofar as a Hispanic lesbian, for example, may have internalized the perspectives of Hispanic culture, of white culture, of straight culture, and of the Catholic church – each viewing her as somehow deficient, but each in different ways. In all of these cases, inner conflict is the result of the internalization of some dominant outlook(s) alongside another outlook that resists the dominant one(s).

There is an older and more inclusive use of the term "double consciousness", however, to describe any state in which one experiences a fundamental clash of perspectives – regardless of the social etiology of those states and regardless of the dominance of one over the other. Ralph Waldo Emerson described a clash between the perspective of reason and the perspective of spirituality as follows:

> The worst feature of this double consciousness is, that the two lives, of the understanding and of the soul, which we lead, really show very little relation to each other, never meet and measure each other: one prevails now, all buzz and din; and the other prevails then, all infinitude and paradise; and, with the progress of life, the two discover no greater disposition to reconcile themselves.
>
> (Emerson 105)

And George Eliot uses the term in a similar way when she presents the suitor Latimer contemplating a marriage with both passion and horror, simultaneously fascinated by the mystery and fearful of the enslavement:

> Are you unable to imagine this double consciousness at work within me, flowing on like two parallel streams that never mingle their waters and blend into a common hue?
>
> (Eliot 21)[3]

In these and similar cases, people can have clashing perspectives on some part of the world – perspectives acquired from different experiences or different languages or different concerns – without one of those perspectives being any more prevalent or any more acceptable than the other. A person's outlook as a naturalist can clash with her outlook as an economist, her New Yorker outlook can clash with her Californian outlook, and her perspective as a mother can clash with her perspective as a judge – creating states of double consciousness where neither side of the opposition is either socially or psychologically dominant over the other.

### CRITERIA AND CLARIFICATION

As I will be using the term, the essential features of double consciousness are the following:

1   A person's experience is organized in accordance with two (or more) *different schemas*.
2   These different schemas are operative at the *same time*, and with respect to the *same situations*.

3    Each of these schemas is *significant* and *lasting*.

4    The use of these different schemas together results in a state of *conscious mental conflict*.

1 A *schema* can be thought of as a framework or a set of guidelines for organizing the information we receive from the world. Schemas foreground some facts and some possibilities while backgrounding others; they guide us to attend to some details and some connections – i.e. some affiliations, some implications – while ignoring others. When hearing a conversation or watching a movie, for example, using a "suspense schema" makes us especially attentive to instances of trust or distrust, to indications of malicious intent, to the risk of dangerous outcomes, and so on. Using a "comedy schema", on the other hand, makes us especially attentive to verbal puns, social gaffs, and the possibility of absurd outcomes. (It was early work on the interpretation of stories that launched what is now an extensive literature on psychological schemas.)[4] Likewise, when observing a married couple, a "romantic schema" makes us more attentive to the expression of affection, more inclined to imagine shared passion, and more confident of a happy ending; whereas an "entrapment schema" makes us more attentive to moments of withdrawal, more inclined to imagine mutual impositions, and more confident of future distress.

The schemas we use for organizing information can be acquired in a variety of ways. Some schemas are given by our biology: we seem to be born with "hunting schemas", "courting schemas", and "parenting schemas", for example – schemas that guide not only our behavior but the way we attend to our surroundings, the patterns we do or do not recognize, and the possibilities we do or do not imagine. These schemas can be elaborated and extended through various kinds of socialization and habituation: an innate hunting schema will be added to and modified by particular hunting practices, and an innate courting schema will be added to and modified by particular courting practices. (These additions and modifications can be thought of as additions and modifications to the strength of certain neural connections.) A child's habits when walking down the street, or when playing with friends, can also create the schemas through which she will experience new neighborhoods and new friends. Language also plays a large role in the creation of information-organizing schemas: different languages highlight different features, create different associations, and invite different inferences. Within each language, furthermore, there will be multiple sublanguages – languages favored by a subset of users, or languages favored in some contexts but not others. "Street language" and "academese" operate in accordance with different schemas insofar as they encourage very different patterns of attention, association, and anticipation.

Individuating schemas, like individuating languages, is not easy. (Is Old English a different language from current English? Is Spanglish a new language? Do I use the same parenting schema as you? Has the younger generation developed a new courting schema?) Fortunately, for our purposes, it is not necessary to decide just when an altered schema becomes a new schema; our interest is directed at cases where the ongoing use of different schemas causes significant mental conflict, where it really doesn't matter whether the conflicting schema count as different versions of the same schema or numerically different schema.

2 Likewise, it is not necessary to be precise about what counts as using different schemas at the *same time* and with respect to the *same situation*. For, again, our focus is on cases

in which the use of different schemas creates a mental conflict, and there will be no psychological conflict unless one experiences the claims of both sides as pertaining to the same domain at the same time. Put another way, it is the subjective sameness of time and the subjective sameness of situation that matters to the experience of (versus the legitimacy of) double consciousness. If Emerson experienced his surroundings through the schema of reason during the week and through the schema of spirituality on the weekend, without either schema operating at the same time, there would be no mental conflict. But he frequently finds himself under the spell of both schemas; thus his inner conflict. Likewise, if Emerson used the schema of reason for dealing with inanimate things and the schema of spirituality for dealing with human things, with no sense of overlap between the two domains, there would not be a mental conflict. But he finds both schemas applicable to most of the things he encounters – animate and inanimate – and inner conflict is the result.

Double consciousness can be avoided, then, by effectively separating the times or the domains in which different schemas are operative. The power of memory and the intermixture of things in the world can make this difficult, however, and, as we will see, the result of such separations may be more harmful than good.

3 There are numerous occasions on which we are torn between two (or more) different ways of understanding a situation and organizing our responses to it: Should I regard a remark as an insult or as a tease? Is the aftermath of a fire starkly beautiful or grimly barren? Is the rejection of an offer an opportunity or a disaster? Was the play a comedy or a tragedy? Most of these occasions are relatively brief and relatively unimportant, however. We quickly opt for one option over the other; or we find an easy

way to diffuse the opposition (teasing includes insults, barren landscapes can be beautiful, disasters provide opportunities, tragic situations can be given a comic presentation); or, often, we simply move on to other concerns. One might regard episodes such as these cases of momentary double consciousness. But I want to reserve the notion of double consciousness for states of inner conflict that are more lasting and more significant. Restricting the term to these weightier cases helps preserve the connection to historic writers such as Du Bois, Emerson, and Eliot (as cited previously). More importantly, though, it justifies talk of a double *consciousness*, or being of two *minds*. For double consciousness involves a mental conflict that is more pervasive and persistent than a person's momentary struggle over how to interpret a remark or how to categorize a movie.

4 The clearest cases of conscious mental conflict are cases where one holds onto beliefs or desires that one knows are *contradictory*. In the case of beliefs, one knows that they can't both be true; in the case of desires, one knows that they can't both be satisfied. (The situation is analogous for expectations, impressions, and recollections—where they are contradictory if it is not possible for both to be true; and with hopes, impulses, and plans—where they are contradictory if it is not possible for both to succeed.) People differ in the degree to which they are bothered by contradictions among their beliefs or desires, but contradictory beliefs or desires generate contradictory dispositions and having contradictory dispositions will be bothersome for anyone. If I believe that the economy will grow while I also believe that the economy will not grow, I experience mental conflict. Likewise, if I desire that the economy will grow while I also desire that the economy will not grow, I experience mental conflict. One way, then, for the use of different schemas to produce an inner conflict

is for them to produce contradictory beliefs or desires. If my reliance on a "neoliberal schema" causes me to believe and to desire that the economy will grow while my reliance on a "Marxist schema" causes me to believe and to desire that the economy will not grow, then using both at the same time will generate an inner conflict. Similarly, if my employment of a "sister schema" causes me to believe that my visitor will be upset by my pain while my employment of a "doctor schema" simultaneously causes me to believe and to desire that she will not be upset, then I will experience an inner conflict.

Contradictions between the beliefs generated by different schemas are not always so obvious. The contradictions between a wave schema for light and a particle schema for light may become evident only when we pursue the implications of each for the passage of light through narrow slots. Or, to take a more ordinary example, a contradiction between my view of you as a good neighbor and my view of you as a traditionalist may become evident only when I start to think about your probable reception of a local immigrant family. Also, we sometimes present our beliefs (to ourselves as well as to others) in ways that cloak their true meaning, making it easier to overlook the contradictions that arise between our various beliefs. When someone says a child is "slow" when they really mean "stupid", it is easier to miss the contradiction that exists between this belief and the belief that IQ rankings are worthless. Or when someone insists that their intention in punishing a child is instruction when it is really revenge, it is easier to ignore the contradiction that exists between that belief about themselves and the belief that they are always loving towards their children. Nevertheless, in many such cases, people will sense an inconsistency in their views. They don't know just where the conflict arises and may not think of it as a latent contradiction, but they feel uncomfortable whenever they contemplate the different ways that they act towards their children, or the different ways that they talk about their neighbors.

It would be a mistake, however, to understand the mental conflict resulting from the use of different schemas solely in terms of the production of contradictory beliefs or desires, whether openly acknowledged or merely sensed. For the very formulation of beliefs and desires generated by one schema tends to differ from the formulation of beliefs and desires generated by another schema, making it difficult to identify claims that are endorsed by one schema and denied by the other. Regarding one's job through the schema of "meaningful work" is unlikely to produce beliefs and desires regarding prizes, while regarding it through the schema of "superior performance" is unlikely to produce beliefs and desires regarding human suffering; it is not the case that one schema produces the belief that one's work is meaningful while the other produces the belief that it is not meaningful, or that one schema produces the belief that a prize is deserved while the other produces the belief that a prize is not deserved. So there is no easy way to identify the "places" where these two schemas conflict. (The same point can be made by considering the use of so-called "thick" concepts – concepts like "puffery" versus "dramatization" or "austere" versus "drab". Each of the concepts in these pairings comes with a rich conceptual surround and it is not easy to identify any particular claim that is affirmed in the application of one concept while denied in the application of the other.) As Emerson states in the passage quoted earlier: "the two lives, of the understanding and of the soul, which we lead, really show very little relation to each other, never meet and measure each other". Yet, when both are active in the same circumstances, we feel the conflict.

It is sometimes said that if two languages, or two schemas, or two cultures are truly incommensurable then no genuine disagreement is possible between them, and any conflict that we experience between them is merely a conflict of power – a conflict over which set of concepts will manage to control the way that people think and act.[5] There is something right and something wrong about this claim. Insofar as using one schema rather than another is a matter of organizing and pursuing information in one way rather than another, then any conflict between schemas must be a conflict between two different ways of doing something (where thinking is itself a kind of doing) – and struggles between two different ways of doing things will be struggles over the allocation of various powers.

Still, insofar as competing schemas share the aim of helping us to understand the world we live in and helping us to thrive in that world, struggles between schemas are something more than struggles over power. They are struggles over how to get things right with respect to the world and our place in it. We want our schemas to do justice to something outside of themselves; we want to understand more about the way the world really is, the way we really feel, the way our institutions really function, the way our interactions with others really work, and so on. The fact that there is no experience that is not already "schematized" in some way or another doesn't mean that there is no world apart from our experience and our schemas, or that the value of a given schema is reducible to its power. We know that the beliefs and desires produced by some schemas will be more revealing and more helpful than the beliefs and desires produced by some other schemas – whether or not we can tell the difference in any given case. So even when the concepts of two different schemas are radically incommensurable, we can experience them as making conflicting claims on us and

*and?* ↙

we can acknowledge that the most powerful schema may not be the schema that is most revealing of the world, or most beneficial to our life in that world.

In sum, we are left with several ways in which our reliance on two (or more) different schemas can produce a mental conflict:

- We might recognize a contradiction between the attitudes produced by one schema and the attitudes produced by another. For example: from one point of view a friend's words seem kind while from another point of view they seem unkind.

- Even though we can't identify any outright contradiction, we might sense that there are contradictions lurking in the background – if only we would follow out the implications more fully, or if only we could be more honest about what we are really thinking. For example: the way a neighbor speaks at meetings doesn't seem to fit with the way she speaks in private, but we can't really say where the conflict lies.

- Using one schema compels us to use our mental resources in one way while using another schema compels us to use those same resources in a different way, so we experience an inner fight over the allocation of mental resources. For example: we have trouble interacting with someone as an employee and at the same time as a friend.

- Even though we find one schema more compelling than another (and we allocate more resources to that schema), we worry that the other schema may be more revealing or more beneficial. For example: we are committed to being a supportive parent but we suspect that our support is unfair to our child's adversary.

As we shall see, different examples of double consciousness involve different types of mental conflict, and different types of mental conflict invite different responses.

## MORE EXAMPLES

Before turning to possible responses to our inner conflicts, it will be helpful to add three more ordinary and contemporary examples of double consciousness to the historical examples of Du Bois, Emerson, and Eliot.

A.  *Spontaneity and Rigor.* Adrian Piper describes the competing perspectives that she holds onto as a philosopher and as an artist as follows: "From the perspective of philosophy, . . . the art community looks undisciplined, impulsive, and gratification-oriented; materialistic, obsessed with the fashion of the moment, and fundamentally unconcerned with standards of quality – which seem to be invoked only as a rationalization for maintaining the status quo of money and power. On the other hand, the art community offers a perspective of untrammeled spontaneity and unpredictability from which . . . the philosophy . . . communities seem staid and controlling, achieving depth and rigor at the expense of inventiveness" (Piper 118–119). Piper considers both the philosophical community and the art community to be guilty of xenophobia, highlighting some similarities between the double consciousness of an African-American as described by Du Bois and the double consciousness of her philosopher-artist identity.[6]

B.  *Trust and Vigilance.* Terry Eagleton offers the following description of double consciousness within the left: "On the one hand, leftists tend to place their faith in certain common decencies and generous impulses. If these were lacking in humanity, it would scarcely be worth the effort of seeking to transform its condition. On the other hand, the left is acutely conscious of just what a catastrophe human history has largely been – a 'sewer', as Jacques Lacan curtly described it. For the most part, the human narrative to date has been one of brutality and injustice, wretchedness and sweated labor. It remains so for many millions in our own time. If it did not, there would be no need to transform the situation as thoroughly as radicals aspire to do. There is no simple contradiction here. If history has been deafened by the din of hacking and gouging, it is partly because violence and scarcity mean that we have not been able to observe men and women at their finest. The faith of the left is that in less burdensome conditions, their creative powers and capacities might have freer rein. It is hard, however, to hold a trust in humanity in tension with a necessary vigilance to the horrors it has manufactured" (Eagleton 37).

C. *Admiration and Dismay*. Many people who live in small towns have developed both a positive outlook and a negative outlook on their community, viewing it through the schema of "personalized interactions", on the one hand, and through the schema of "passive belligerence", on the other. They praise the laid-back nature of public life in their town, but bemoan its ineptness. They admire the gritty directness of the local schoolyard but cringe at the lack of oversight. The small houses are cozy and unpretentious but also neglected and sad. There is something endearingly kooky about the costumed skaters but the emotional atmosphere is deadening. (City dwellers, of course, have similarly contrasting views of their cities.) There is nothing surprising or uncomfortable about liking some things and disliking other things about one's town. But here it is the very same things that prompt opposed reactions: the very same interactions with a clerk, or a mayor, will seem pleasantly laid back *and* deliberately obtuse; the very same schoolyard fight will seem admirably direct *and* worrisomely unregulated; the very same skaters will seem wonderfully kooky *and* lacking in spirit. Townsfolk might flip back and forth between the opposing views, but an inner tension frequently persists; for even if one outlook dominates for a time, the opposing view will often linger.[7]

With these everyday examples added to the examples described by Du Bois, Emerson, and Eliot, we can now consider arguments for, and arguments against, remaining in a state of double consciousness, continuing to be of two minds.

*do problems*

## THE PROS AND CONS OF HOLDING ONTO DOUBLE CONSCIOUSNESS

Quarrels with ourselves, like quarrels with others, can add to our knowledge, improve our relations with others, and allow us to live more authentic lives. Quarrels allow for the expression of opposing points of view, and that gives alternative perspectives a "voice". Quarrels cause us to challenge our assumptions, and that can make us dig deeper, revealing new facts and new possibilities.[8] Also, odd as it may seem, quarrels can lead to improvements in the way we interact with other people – causing us to be more honest with each other and forcing us to find better ways to accommodate different priorities and different vulnerabilities. Still, defending the value of a quarrel is not the same as defending the value of a persistent, unending quarrel – especially when that quarrel is a quarrel with ourselves. Occasional quarrels may be beneficial, but how can we improve our knowledge and our relationships if we are quarrelling all of the time?

The first thing to note is that voicing one's dissent can be valuable even if it slows the road to knowledge and even if it damages interpersonal relations. There are many different defenses of freedom of expression and only some of these turn on its (eventual) contributions to social harmony. The more one thinks in terms of individual rights rather than social outcomes, for example, the more one wants to ensure that every voice, right or wrong, continues to have a recognized standing, that every point of view continues to have a place in the forum of public opinion. Even when one thinks in terms of outcomes rather than rights, however, and even if one prioritizes the good of social harmony, one could defend the value of ongoing quarrels on the grounds that dissent cannot be eliminated, it can only be suppressed, and the suppression of dissent will eventually lead to a society that is more violent and more conflicted than a society that accepts ongoing quarrels. The idea is that excluded or defeated parties to a quarrel will eventually return to cause even more trouble. Arguments along this line have been buttressed by psychoanalytic theories about the ill effects of impulse suppression, by literary theories about the inevitable eruptions of what remains unsaid, and by various accounts of the political functioning of "abject" positions.[9] One doesn't need to claim that all ways of bringing quarrels to an end, or all ways of achieving social harmony, will backfire in order to see how this is at least sometimes the case and that ongoing quarreling can sometimes serve social harmony better than any available way of ending the quarrel.

Equally, quarrels do not have to end in order to advance our knowledge. John Stuart Mill's notable defense of free speech – as the best way to bring new facts to light – did not assume that such revelations would put an end to the quarreling. He argued that we can never be entirely certain of the truth of our beliefs, but that continuing to welcome and engage with dissent is the best way to increase our confidence while also acknowledging the impossibility of certainty (Mill 39–40). In the legal domain there are various practical reasons to secure an end to a quarrel (limits on personal and state resources, the need to protect people from further violence, the need to clear someone's name, and so on). But it is easy to imagine how an endless trial, with endlessly sparring lawyers, could continue to bring more and more facts to light. And in medical research, that is frequently what happens; opposing approaches to the treatment of cancer, for example, continue to reveal new facts about our bodies and our environments without any promise of bringing those quarrels to an end. The revelation of new facts and overlooked considerations can be valuable even if we are never able to see how everything fits together into a coherent whole. Indeed, attempts at achieving wholeness can sometimes prevent us from making important discoveries.[10]

When it comes to interpersonal relations, it might seem that quarrels must come to an end before effective action is possible, but there are some cases in which the continued reliance on conflicting schemas actually extends rather than restricts the effectiveness of joint endeavors. Parents may have conflicting views about what their role as parents should be – one focused on taming otherwise wild behavior, the other focused on encouraging an adventurous outlook, but the end result of the parental conflict may be a child that is less wild and more adventurous (perhaps because the adventurousness provides an outlet for otherwise wild impulses). Likewise, within politics, the fact that some view unemployment compensation as a right while others view it as a gift might actually add to the likelihood that changes that appeal to both parties will be enacted. Furthermore, insofar as improvements in our interactions with others depend on each party *not* acting on their aims (not going to war, for example, or not undermining another person's ambitions), the persistence of conflict can be a good thing. In our personal lives, as in politics, we ought to be wary of those who insist that "we must do something" or that "anything is better than nothing" – for that often encourages actions that are not only misguided, they are unreliable and in that sense they are irresponsible actions.[11]

Ongoing conflicts within ourselves can seem more problematic. Acceptance or encouragement of a quarrelsome society comes more easily than acceptance or encouragement of a quarrelsome self. Why is this? There are some interesting philosophical arguments to the effect that *significant, ongoing* perspectival conflicts within *oneself* (what I have been calling states of double consciousness), are either impossible or undesirable. Thinking through this array of arguments should help clarify what is assumed, what is denied, and what is implied by my defense of inner quarrels.

One set of arguments, developed by Immanuel Kant, maintains that the only way for a conscious subject to continue across time is for the contents of its experience to continue across time. But given the constant flux of information we receive, the only way for the contents of experience to continue across time is for that information to be organized in such a way that different impressions are recognized as appearances of the same objects – the same objects viewed from different angles, registered through different senses, encountered at different times. According to Kant, subject awareness and object awareness go hand-in-hand; there is no self-awareness apart from our awareness of the way in which the very same objects can appear to us in different ways – depending on when and where we are located, whether we are looking or just listening, and so on.

One does not need to follow, or agree with, the details of Kant's arguments in order to acknowledge a close connection between unifying the contents of experience and unifying the subject of experience. Does this mean that using different schemas for organizing our experience – using conflicting sets of concepts and conflicting projections to understand our surroundings – results in the creation of different subjects? This will depend on the extent and the depth of the divide. In the cases of double consciousness that we will be considering, there are conflicting ways of categorizing people, events, or places but there remains agreement about which people, events, and places are being described (this population, that comment, that town); likewise, there are conflicting views about what causes what but there remains agreement about which things need to be explained (this behavior, that outcome, that change). These categories – person, place, event – are thin rather than thick concepts, but they are not empty; they provide the grounding that is necessary for even recognizing a disagreement as such. We experience the world as spatiotemporally continuous even if we are divided over the nature of its properties and the structure of its causes. Thus the basic Kantian requirements for a single subject of consciousness are met, even though that subject may continue to rely on conflicting conceptual schemas and continue to experience double consciousness as a result.

The requirements for being a single *self* may be stronger than the requirements for being a single *subject* of experience. In addition to experiencing the world as a spatiotemporally continuous world, having a self may depend on achieving the kind of integration of judgments that makes rational thought and rational action possible. Infants, for example, may experience the world as a continuous whole (for long stretches of time, anyway) without yet being capable of rational action in that world and, in that sense, without yet having a self. On this understanding of what it takes to be a self, double consciousness threatens selfhood by threatening the rational integration of thoughts and actions. Insofar as it prevents one from thinking and acting in a fully rational way, it diminishes one's selfhood, and insofar as it causes one to operate with two distinct rationalities, it creates two distinct selves.

Some degree of rationality is required for us to have any beliefs and desires. For beliefs and desires are the attitudes that make sense of a person's behavior, that make that person's behavior seem rational from their point of view. Determining what a person believes and desires depends, therefore, on determining how they are likely to behave. We may not know whether a person, including ourselves, really believes that their neighbors are trustworthy or really believes that they are dangerous until we see how that person acts around those neighbors. And we may not know whether people, including ourselves, intend good or ill until we observe their behavior across a range of cases. (The relevant behavior should include verbal behavior − what we *say* about our neighbors, for example; and it should include behavior that is emotionally expressive − facial expressions, for example.) The effects of our beliefs and desires on behavior need not be immediate or direct, however, so a person's failure to do anything in response to an imminent danger might not indicate indifference so much as an inner conflict between contradictory inclinations. (Buridan's ass was not indifferent to food; it was conflicted between two equally tempting options.) There is no simple argument, then, from the impossibility of contradictory actions to the impossibility of contradictory beliefs and desires.

It is possible, of course, for a self to shift from one point of view to another – from one religious outlook to another, for example, or from one conception of a family to another. But the continuity of a self (versus a mere subject) requires that these changes are rationally intelligible transitions rather than arbitrary fluctuations. If, on the basis of assorted observations and reflections, I shift from believing that there is a single all-powerful god to believing that there are many gods with very limited powers, then I will have undergone a shift in schema whereby it can be difficult to describe the conflict in any neutral way (what does "god" even mean? what makes a god "good"?). But as long as the shift is rationally intelligible – a case of beliefs and desires trying to make sense of available information – then it doesn't undermine the rational continuity of a self. Likewise, if you entertain conflicting conceptions of a family, temporarily unable to choose between the two conceptions, there is no threat to you having a rationally unified self (indeed, the ability to contemplate competing conceptions may be an important contribution to one's rationality). But can I continue to adhere to conflicting religious outlooks, and can you continue to endorse conflicting conceptions of a family, and still count as a rational self?

What is wrong with having a diminished self – less integration and more spontaneity, less ego and more id? And why shouldn't we enjoy having more than one self? There are at least two possible answers to these questions. First, there is the claim that achieving greater coordination among our beliefs and desires enhances our coordination with the world – the eradication of contradictions making it more likely that our beliefs are true and more likely that our desires can be satisfied. If we allow our beliefs to pull us in too many directions, we are less likely to converge on the truth; and if we allow our desires to pull us in too many directions, we are less likely to find satisfaction. Second, there is the claim that more fully integrated selves are more responsible selves – being answerable to a larger set of judgments and actions and accepting responsibility for more of the past and future. When there is a lack of rational continuity between different aspects of a person's behavior, whether past or present, it is easier for a person to disown some of those behaviors (and it is easier for a society to absolve that individual of responsibility for the aberrant behavior). Claims about the desirability of wholeheartedness are particularly evident in discussions of love, where inner conflict is viewed as particularly worrisome. Harry Frankfurt, for example, writes "Love makes it possible for us to engage wholeheartedly in activity that is meaningful" (90) and "The pure heart is the heart of someone who is volitionally unified, and who is thus fully intact. . . . Deficiency in wholeheartedness is a kind of irrationality, then, which infects our practical lives and renders them incoherent" (96). Praise for wholeheartedness also pervades much of what is said to students about choosing a career (Chang), to believers about adhering to their faith, and to parents about choosing to have children (Paul).

There are good reasons to favor more integrated selves in general, but there are important exceptions and it is the exceptions that I want to focus on. With respect to the first reason in favor of rational integration – the promise of improved coordination with the world – there are cases where the maintenance of conflicting beliefs, however awkward, offers a truer view of the world than what is offered by any available resolution of the conflict; and there are cases where the maintenance of conflicting desires, however uncomfortable, offers a better chance of personal satisfaction than any realistic elimination of the conflict. With respect to the second reason in favor of rational integration – the increase in personal responsibility that it makes possible – there are cases where double consciousness enables one to be more rather than less responsible for one's thoughts and one's behavior.

Consider some of the previously described examples of double consciousness. By maintaining the perspective of an artist and the perspective of a philosopher, Piper thinks that she acquires more knowledge about the world not only because each perspective reveals more aspects of the world but also because each perspective illuminates the other's shortcomings – shortcomings that are inseparable from the insights offered by each. It is not possible, in her opinion, to meld the opposing perspectives together into a coherent whole without a loss of insight. Her own sense of fulfillment, furthermore, depends on cultivating both perspectives; while the pursuit of her artistic aims and the pursuit of her philosophic aims are in clear conflict, her personal satisfaction depends on her continuing to pursue both. And while her missing of deadlines and her absences from the classroom may seem to indicate a failure to take responsibility for her actions, she seems quite ready to take responsibility for her actions – willingly forgoing lucrative commissions and a tenured professorship. Eagleton also thinks that a combination of trust and despair serves to show us more of the truth about humanity and enables us to act more successfully for its betterment – not in spite of the conflict but because of the conflict. Indeed, he suggests that the tension between the two perspectives is needed to keep us honest about the human condition and to keep us trying to better that condition. This uneasy combination of trust and despair might also be said to enhance, rather than detract from, our sense of responsibility for the human condition (as trust alone, or despair alone, would lead to seeing less and doing less).

## ENDING A QUARREL

Are Piper and Eagleton (and Du Bois and Emerson and Eliot), with their embrace of double consciousness, overlooking preferable alternatives – alternatives that would eliminate the states of double consciousness that they describe (and that they suffer from) without shortchanging the insights of each perspective?

The most satisfying way of ending a conflict is through some sort of resolution. Resolutions achieve agreement between the opponents, creating or restoring a sense of harmony between the previously quarreling parties. We can group resolutions into three categories: concessions, subsumptions, and supersessions – or, in more colloquial language, mutual agreement that one of the two parties is correct and the other not, mutual agreement that one of the two positions actually covers or includes the other, or mutual agreement on a third position.

In none of the previous examples does a resolution by concession seem appropriate. Each of the opposed points of view have something valuable to offer: the perspective of the educated and the perspective of the laborer (for Du Bois), the perspective of science and the perspective of the soul (for Emerson), the perspective of passion and the perspective of autonomy (for Eliot), the perspective of the artist and the perspective of the philosopher (for Piper), the perspective of trust and the perspective of vigilance (for Eagleton), and the perspective of admiration and the perspective of dismay (for the small town resident). Something important would be lost if any of these perspectives were rejected outright.

More promising, perhaps, is the possibility of resolution through subsumption – the fitting of one set of insights under the umbrella of the other. Could the knowledge one gains as a laborer be subsumed by academic theories (or vice versa)? Could a science of the mind include an understanding of the soul (or vice versa)? Could the perspective of passion encompass the perspective of autonomy (or vice versa)? Could artistic insights be subsumed under philosophical insights (or vice versa)? And so on. Hopeful as these subsumptions sound in the abstract, their success is implausible as a matter of empirical fact. They are not true to the experience of those who work in the fields while attending college; for those workers do not view their work as a part of their theorizing. They are not true to the experience of those who search for the meaning of their lives in the study of artificial intelligence or neurology; for such people are inevitably disappointed by science's failure to provide guidance in their most important decisions. They are not true to the experience of those who pursue careers in both philosophy and art. And so on. As a matter of empirical fact, then, we are left with people who adopt one perspective rather than the other, or people who hold onto both perspectives but continue to experience a conflict between the two. This is not, I suggest, because of any failure in people's attention or reasoning – a failure to realize that one perspective is really just an aspect of the other. Rather, it is a reflection of the very real but competing insights of alternative perspectives. It is not possible to fit the knowledge gained through one schema into the knowledge gained through the other.

What about resolution through supersession – through the formulation of some third, more inclusive option? This seems to be the hope of Du Bois, for example, when he aspires to a greater synthesis of the competing perspectives of African-Americans.[12] He envisions a new, evolved human being who is able to draw on the knowledge gained by the competing perspectives of his African and his American heritage to create a more ideal unity:

> the ideal of human brotherhood, gained through the unifying ideal of Race; the ideal of fostering and developing the traits and talents of the Negro, not in opposition to or contempt for other races, but rather in large conformity to the greater ideals of the American Republic, in order that some day on American soil two world-races may give each to each those characteristics both so sadly lack.
>
> (7)

In the years since Du Bois wrote this passage, we have become more wary of the purported neutrality or universality of the "greater ideals of the American Republic" – ideals such as freedom of choice and equality of opportunity, where appeal to these ideals has often justified precisely the sort of laissez-faire economics that increases inequality and enforces conformity to the dominant norms. Again, this is a problem for any ideal at this level of abstraction: it provides a word and image ("human brotherhood") that is supposed to guide our thoughts and actions, but the application of this word and image is so underspecified that they are nearly useless as guides (and worse than useless insofar as they divert us from more detailed distinctions and decisions). None of this excludes either the possibility or the desirability of overcoming the sort of double consciousness that Du Bois describes. But it raises serious doubts about the possibility of surmounting the conflict of perspectives through appeals to "freedom", "equality", or "human brotherhood".

We encounter exactly the same problem, I suggest, if we attempt to overcome the conflict between our outlooks on a small town by replacing them with a third, more inclusive outlook. While the schemas of "personalized interactions" and "passive belligerence" highlight different patterns in the behavior of town folk, schemas that offer to locate these patterns within a more encompassing third pattern – the schema of "a self-protective community", for example, or the schema of "a conservative backwater" – are likely to be overly abstract, draining our previous observations of their specificity and their "bite". (The same holds for attempts to unify the perspective of an artist and the perspective of a philosopher under the umbrella of "critical engagement" or "creative inquiry".) It is a bit like viewing a complex mosaic through incompatible frameworks – on the one hand, as a set of stars, on the other hand, as a set of octagons – and seeking to overcome the opposition by appeal to the more general schema of "geometrical"; the third schema supersedes the others and overcomes the conflict between them, but only by ignoring many of the details that were revealed by the two initial schemas.

A second, perhaps more common way of ending a quarrel is through some sort of *separation*. We can group separations into two categories: practical separations and conceptual separations. Practical separations occur when we eliminate conflict by drawing a clear line between the domains or times within which competing perspectives shall have dominion. Lines could be drawn between physical domains, between social contexts, between tasks, or simply between times. These separations often serve to restore the peace and allow the practicalities of life to proceed smoothly. Piper maintains a separation between her artist friends and her philosopher friends and between her artistic projects and her philosophical projects. Emerson seems to have kept his scientific endeavors separate from his spiritual endeavors. Eagleton moves forward with optimism but looks back with pessimism. But these are ways of side-stepping rather than resolving disagreements, and they foster tolerance, not harmony. Each of these writers is aware of the conflict that results from bringing both schemas to bear on the same things, and none of them suggest that one schema is more appropriate than the other with respect to those things. (Piper values the artist's take on philosophy and the philosopher's take on art, Emerson looks at the very same woods through the perspective of a scientist and the perspective of a spiritualist, and Eagleton recognizes the legitimacy of pessimism *and* optimism with respect to both the past *and* the future of humanity.) Yet they diffuse the inner conflict they feel by maintaining a practical separation between their competing outlooks.

In addition to practical separations, there are conceptual separations that foster tolerance rather than harmony. An extreme defense of conceptual separation is that of radical relativists, who insist that beliefs and desires are only true or appropriate relative to the specific situation of a particular subject at a particular time. If the perspective of a subject changes over time or differs across contexts, there is no real disagreement since the judgments that come with each perspective will never be about the same things. The thoughts and actions of one person may offend or interfere with the thoughts or actions of another person, of course, and in this sense there can be conflict; but realizing the incommensurability of the two views, and in the absence of any higher court of appeals, the only appropriate response may be an attitude of tolerance. There are also less radical attempts at conceptual separation. Philosophers are particularly good at finding ways to circumvent apparent contradictions – introducing distinctions or adding qualifications until no real contradiction remains. And that can bring an end to conflict. Still, there is a danger here in cutting things too finely, not just logically but psychologically: our thinking and our acting are not and cannot be nuanced beyond a certain point. Our thinking and acting depend on discerning patterns in our surroundings, and although those patterns can be more rather than less fine-grained, they cannot be infinitely fine-grained.

A third and final way of ending a quarrel is through *dissolution*, which can be achieved through intentional attempts at distraction or a more or less passive acquiescence to the passage of time. Dissolutions (as I am using the term) end with a kind of forgetfulness or agreement to move on. Unlike resolutions, dissolutions do not conclude in a sense of mutual satisfaction; and unlike separations, they do not end in a mutual respect for boundaries. If you think my remark was offensive and I think it was penetrating, we may argue for a time and then seek to distract ourselves from our argument – not only for the sake of temporary relief from stress, but also with the hope that we will eventually forget the grounds for our disagreement and thereby remove the very possibility of continuing our quarrel. Or, even if we remember and retain grounds for a disagreement, those grounds will come to have a less significant place in our lives and the original disagreement will no longer bother us. The same thing can happen to the quarrels we have with ourselves. A person who views marriage through the competing lenses of passion and confinement may decide in favor of marriage (or against) and simply wait for the opposing view to lose its grip – to disappear with time, to shrivel up from neglect. Citizens of a small town might find it more comfortable to retain a positive view of their community and may choose to "close their eyes" to the negative. And so on for the other examples we have discussed. The downside of such dissolutions, of course, is the loss of knowledge made available through the abandoned perspective. The married person no longer recognizes what they have lost; the citizen no longer sees what is bad in her community; the optimistic liberal becomes blind to human ugliness. While it might be argued that losing that knowledge enables one to more fully pursue the knowledge offered by the preserved perspective, the loss is undeniable. And while it might be argued that single-mindedness enables one to act with more confidence, it is hard to defend confidence that depends on a kind of willed ignorance.

I am not claiming that inner conflicts should always be tolerated, and I have not argued against every option for ending each of the conflicts described in this chapter. I do hope to have shown how continuing to be of two minds is often preferable to the alternatives, however. (Subsequent chapters carry the argument further, describing some especially fundamental instances of desirable double consciousness.)

## MODELS FOR SUSTAINING A CONFLICT

I end this chapter by introducing three different models for sustaining double consciousness. It is not comfortable to live in a state of inner conflict, but there are more or less graceful, more or less helpful, and more or less enjoyable ways of living with a double consciousness.

The first model is the *juggling* model. Gloria Anzaldua writes:

> The new mestiza copes by developing a tolerance for contradictions, a tolerance for ambiguity. She learns to be an Indian in Mexican culture, to be a Mexican from an Anglo point of view. She learns to juggle cultures. She has a plural personality, she operates in a pluralistic mode – nothing is thrust out, the good the bad the ugly, nothing rejected nothing abandoned. Not only does she sustain contradictions, she turns the ambivalence into something else.
>
> *what?*
>
> (Anzaldua 79)[13]

Here Anzaldua emphasizes her split loyalties – the continuing ambivalence she feels in the face of the contradictions that come with being Indian and Mexican, Mexican and Anglo. What is good from one perspective is bad from another, and what is appropriate in one culture is inappropriate in another. Any attempt at eliminating the conflicts would involve a loss of some valuable parts of alternate cultures (losses that are seldom evenly distributed among the unified cultures); better to work with the contradictions than to try and eliminate them. This is a classic case of inner conflict due to one's position within conflicting cultures but Anzaldua, unlike Du Bois, doesn't wish for a final synthesis of conflicting cultures. Instead, the reference to juggling suggests extreme adeptness at moving between cultures – back and forth, first one and then the other balanced in one's hand. More than that, however, it recognizes the extent to which the nature of our engagement with a given culture depends on the opposing demands of other cultures to which we belong. The way we engage with our Anglo identity is affected by the fact that we also have a Mexican identity – just as the way that we engage with a given ball is determined by what other balls are in the air. The juggler stays attuned to her multiple balls, not resolving their conflicting demands so much as keeping them in a kind of free-play, continually finding ways to keep each ball (i.e. each part of her identity) active despite the competition.

The preceding quoted passage ends with the promise that the cultural juggler turns her ambivalence into "something else" – presumably something more desirable than mere ambivalence between two options. Anzaldua does not seek some new sort of unity – some way of living in harmony with oneself after all. Instead she seems to anticipate the emergence of new experiences, new behaviors, and new opportunities that actually depend on the continuation of the conflicts. The "new mestiza" savors her contradictions (much as we might savor the combination of sweet and sour, or bitter and sweet) and she finds new ways of being in the world as a result. Surely, there are numerous ways in which opposing experiences or roles (Anglo and Mexican, male and female, child and parent, counselor and comedian) can be combined – without eliminating their opposition – to create something new.

Adrian Piper offers a similar model for relishing states of double consciousness when she compares her wearing of "three hats" to the creation of polyphonic music:

> [The] relation between all three kinds of cycles of work can be compared to the process of recording and mixing an early Renaissance mass by Johannes Ockeghem. Ockeghem's method of composition was polyphonic,

in which each voice or instrument was scored to a different melody, and all played more or less simultaneously. . . . Listening to this kind of composition is a little like mixing it in the recording studio: within an ongoing, complex band of sound, you can hear different, ongoing strands of melody that sometimes combine to form chords, or separate to form counterpoint. You can tune in to one — i.e. turn up its volume, and bring it into the foreground. The others continue, but more quietly, in the background. Then that one may return to the background, while the volume goes up on two others, and you hear the shifting sequences of chords and counterpoint they form in combination. And sometimes you can hear all of the individual melodies, chords, and counterpoints, distinctly and in partial and full combination, even though all are playing simultaneously. When that happens you are floating in a billowing, rushing stream of sound, composed of rivulets of voice and instrumentation. Then you just relax, and let it carry you wherever it will.

(127)[14]

A second model for sustaining inner conflict is the isometrics model. Isometrics is a form of exercise in which two sets of muscles push or pull against each other in order to strengthen each other. Similarly, in the case of cultural conflict, one might continue an inner quarrel not only to preserve one's various cultural affinities but also to strengthen each side of the opposition. If one part of our heritage values reticence and another values assertiveness, keeping the opposition clearly in mind can actually strengthen our allegiance to each. Insofar as the ongoing presence of an internal opponent helps to highlight the "contours" of a given position (just as the resistance of an opposing force helps to highlight the contours of a given muscle), it strengthens our ability to use that position (that "muscle") effectively.

In addition to strengthening competing forces, isometric oppositions can add to one's stability. When an arm stretching off to the right is countered by an arm stretching off to the left, a more stable center is secured. Something similar can happen in the case of inner psychological conflicts, where the tension created by attitudes pulling in opposite directions can actually stabilize our outlook, making us more rather than less grounded. Inner conflict, openly pursued, can stabilize our actions as well. This is a familiar theme in psychotherapy, where the (often dangerous) instability of people's actions is frequently attributed to their inability to tolerate inner conflict.[15] Such people tend to throw themselves into one pursuit after another, each pursuit eventually undermined by the eruption of countervailing forces that were suppressed or ignored.[16] Their relationships tend to be wracked by unpredictable fluctuations between total attachment and total rejection.[17] Parents who can feel simultaneously angry and loving (simultaneously disgusted and amused, simultaneously skeptical and trusting) towards their child are less likely to flip back and forth between the two attitudes, less likely to have excessive responses, and less likely to feel either confused or guilty about their feelings. A marriage can be more stable when spouses allow themselves to have contradictory impulses and feelings – towards each other and towards the marriage itself – rather than denying or diverting critical perspectives, and rather than see-sawing back and forth between competing outlooks. Needless to say, being a responsible person depends on being a reliable person; others must be able to count on the outcomes of our promises and plans. In at least some cases, then, the fact that we continue to quarrel with ourselves adds to rather than detracts from our status as responsible agents.

Applying this model to the case of Eagleton's liberal, who adheres to a schema of trust alongside a schema of vigilance, it is easy to see how their inner quarrel, like many outer quarrels, can increase the strength of each position – by forcing each side to produce more evidence and more reasoning in its own defense. Retaining both perspectives, despite their evident conflict, also allows the liberal to continue to act in a more reliable, more sustainable way.

A third model for sustaining inner conflict is the disrupter model. Whereas the previous juggling model and isometrics model are both ways of handling inner conflicts that already exist, the disrupter model is a way of destabilizing a comfortable position, a way of generating inner conflicts that didn't previously exist – or, more exactly, conflicts of which one was not previously aware. (That said, the line between previously nonexistent and previously unnoticed inner conflicts can be unclear, especially if one holds the view that any meaning whatsoever depends on the "shadow presence" of its opposite.) Shakespeare and other authors often introduce fools to play this role – undermining those in power by mocking their most cherished assumptions.[18] Philosophers are often trained for this role insofar as they are trained to "play the devil's advocate" – not just raising doubts but actively arguing for the opposite of any significant claim. If someone claims that we live in a physical world, argue that actually only minds exist. If someone claims that suffering is bad, argue that suffering is actually good. If someone claims that ideas precede words, argue that words actually precede ideas. The tactic is familiar and, if successful, it creates a conscious conflict where there

*good? ?*
*bad ?*

previously was none. Usually the rationale for such interventions, like the rationale for opposing lawyers, is that strenuous opposition is the best way to disclose the truth. It may also serve to instill some needed humility. A further aim of deconstructionism, largely due to Jacques Derrida, is to counter the concentration of power that accrues to any dominant discourse – by defending opposing interpretations of whatever is said. Within this school of thought, the aim of such inversions is not the discovery of some further truth (nor the furthering of humility, nor an increase in stability) but, rather, resistance to the dominant discourse, whatever that discourse may be; it is a move against any concentration of power, whenever and wherever it occurs. Finally, regardless of their truth, previously undisclosed perspectives – especially those that turn received views on their head – tend to be more interesting to us, and being interesting is another goal for the perpetual disrupter.

We can, of course, act as our own disrupter – perpetually challenging our own assumptions and upending our own concentrations of power. The admirer of a small town can cultivate a more disparaging perspective (or vice versa). The scientist can go out of her way to sympathize with those who reject science. The spiritualist can go out of her way to advance a materialist point of view. Unlike the model of juggling or the model of isometrics which offer ways of living with conflict more comfortably and with greater stability, this model assumes that one or another schema will always manage to become dominant and that domination by any one schema is inherently bad (epistemologically, morally, or aesthetically). It has us perpetually on guard, therefore, against the accumulation of power to any one view and it remains committed to disrupting that power through the cultivation of conflicting schemas.

This is not an exhaustive list of possible styles or models for sustaining inner conflict. But it suggests some less painful, more productive ways that we might continue to quarrel with ourselves – in order to preserve the integrity and richness of different parts of ourselves, or in order to achieve greater stability with ourselves and with others, or in order to diffuse a concentration of power and mobilize suppressed energy. The following chapters consider how each of these models might suit other important cases of double consciousness.

# Two

> With memory set smarting like a reopened wound, a man's past is not simply a dead history, an outworn preparation of the present: it is not a repented error shaken loose from the life: it is a still quivering part of himself, bringing shudders and bitter flavors and the tinglings of a merited shame.
>
> (Eliot, chapter LXI)

This passage, from George Eliot's *Middlemarch*, captures something important about the way that vivid memories can disrupt our present experience – not just by interrupting the flow of thoughts focused on one's present, but by creating a kind of double perspective on one's present. The passage concerns the character Mr. Balstrode, who has made a series of decisions that seem reprehensible according to his earlier moral schema but justifiable according to his subsequent moral schema. Balstrode does not just remember his past and now regret it; rather, he calls up the perspective of his youth, experiences its clash with his more recent perspective, and is now inwardly torn. His memories reactivate his past self and the perspective of that past self becomes a "quivering part" of his present self as well, bringing "shudders and bitter flavors" into that present self. The result is a distinctive sort of double consciousness – one which, in many cases, is worth retaining.

Many philosophers have claimed that the boundaries of our selves are determined, at least in part, by the boundaries of our memories.[1] What I can no longer remember thinking or doing is no longer part of my self (and, perhaps, no longer something I can be held responsible for).[2] Many objections have been raised about this position: objections to restricting the self to what is conscious, objections to the circularity of using continuities of memory to determine what counts as a self while also using continuity of selves to determine what counts as a memory, and objections to the emphasis on memory versus other forms of psychological continuity.[3] These are all disputes about the role of memory in the continuation of selves across time. The questions I will be pursuing, on the other hand, are questions about how we experience our memories – in particular, how certain types of memory can give rise to a valuable form of double consciousness.

## EPISODIC MEMORIES AND IMAGINED FUTURES

The memories I am interested in are usually called "episodic" or "autobiographical" memories. (The terms are misleading since they need not be fleeting and they may not be about one-self.) The important thing about these memories is that they revive or recreate an experience from the first-person point of view. One doesn't just remember *that* one walked through a field of lavender or *that* one used to enjoy loud rock music. One *relives* the walk – looking out over the field from five feet above the ground, smelling the dry fragrance of the lavender, noticing how the color seems to blur at the horizon; or one *relives* the thrill of rock's pounding beat – the awakened desire, the spirit of rebellion, the sense of being a part of something much bigger than oneself. Such memories need not be entirely accurate,[4] but they must give one the sense of being "there" all over again. Episodic memories are often contrasted with "semantic" or "factual" or "general" memories – memories that such and such happened but without any reactivation of a first-person point of view on the remembered event. (The terms are again misleading since semantic memories need not be retained in words, they may not be entirely accurate, and they can be about very particular things.[5]) Most of our memories combine these two sorts of memory, and it is not uncommon for one sort to slip into the other, but the distinction is a useful one (both philosophically and scientifically).[6]

A nice example of episodic memory can be found in Proust's description of an aging Marcel who trips and recovers his balance, causing him to relive a series of previous experiences and, more importantly, to revive a previous frame of mind:

> as I moved sharply backwards I tripped against the uneven paving-stones in front of the coach-house. And at the moment when, recovering my balance, I put my foot on a stone which was slightly lower than its neighbor, all my discouragement vanished and in its place was that same happiness which at various epochs of my life had been given to me by the sight of trees which I had thought I recognized in the course of a drive near Balbec, by the sight of the twin steeples of Martinville, by the flavour of a madeleine dipped in tea, and by all those last works of Vinteuil had seemed to me to combine the quintessential character. Just as, at the moment when I tasted the madeleine, all anxiety about the future, all intellectual doubts had disappeared, so now those that a few seconds ago had assailed me on the subject of the reality of my literary gifts, the reality even of literature, were removed as if by magic.
>
> (Proust 255–256)

When we relive a past experience from the first-person point of view – reexperiencing the shapes and colors of the lavender field, reexperiencing the excitement of listening to rock music, or reexperiencing the taste of the madeleine – we can occupy two different perspectives, the perspective recaptured in the memory together with the perspective of one's present. I am not referring to the fact that the remembered point of view is directed at a lavender field or at rock music or at a madeleine while one's current point of view is directed at a desk or a telephone or a paving stone; that is a difference in the object of attention, not in the schema through which one experiences a particular event. The relevant contrast is, rather, the contrast between one's past perspective on the field or the music or one's life and one's present perspective on the field or the music or one's life. From one's present perspective the rock music might seem sappy and crass, which conflicts with one's past view of it as wild and profound. Alternatively, one might now regard certain rock music as a finely calibrated creation where one once experienced it as simple triggers for animal responses. Either way, vividly recalling the past experience can prompt a kind of uneasy discomfort.

The tension between one's past perspective and one's present perspective will be lesser or greater depending on how much they differ and depending on how important the difference is. Vivid memories of walking through a field of lavender or listening to a rock concert or eating a madeleine, disorienting as they may be, are not likely to create a significant and sustained conflict in the way one schematizes one's experience; so they do not result in significant sorts of double consciousness. Eliot's Mr. Balstrode, on the other hand, is continually plagued by a very significant contrast between the righteous convictions of his past ("He believed without effort in the peculiar work of grace within him") and his later acceptance of the pragmatics of success in business:

> Night and day, without interruption save of brief sleep which only wove retrospect and fear into a fantastic present, he felt the scenes of his earlier life coming between him and everything else, as obstinately as, when we look through the window from a lighted room, the objects we turn our back on are still before us, instead of the grass and the trees. The successive events, inward and outward, were there in one view: though each might be dwelt on in turn the rest still kept their hold in the consciousness.
>
> (chapter LXI)

Balstrode exemplifies a kind of double consciousness that is actually quite common. Many people continue to be haunted by the contrast between their idealistic past and their conventional present, between the headlong enthusiasm of their past self and the wary caution of their present self, or between the unconditional character of a past commitment and the more calculating character of a present commitment. Others are haunted by the contrast between their extremely reasonable past self and their carefree present self, or between a past sense of belonging in society and a present sense of living on its outskirts (or vice versa). From the point of view of one's past self, the fact that one has become a lawyer, or that one's child is living at home, may appear wonderful or it may represent failure (depending on the expectations and values one had in the past). While the (semantic) memory that one used to view things differently is unlikely to create an inner conflict, the (episodic) memory of what it was like to view things in that way brings the conflict to life and engenders a distinctive sort of tension in one's present experience.

Shame and disapproval (or pride and admiration) can point in both directions; one's past can look shameful (or admirable) from the perspective of one's present *and* one's present can look shameful from the perspective of one's past. Balstrode's self-serving business decisions merit shame when viewed from the perspective of his idealistic past, and the righteous pronouncements of his past merit shame when viewed from the perspective of his pragmatic present. (Such symmetries of shame do not require that the two instances of shame are equally strong or equally valid.) The shame he feels is not just directed at past or present actions, it is directed at the person that he once was or the person that he now is. The result is a present experience of a deep conflict between past self and present self.

The conflict between past and present selves can be powerful without being painful. Tessa Hadley has written many short stories about our uneasy yet gratifying relation to past points of view. She describes her own experience of rereading a favorite childhood story as follows:

> It's a strange experience to reread a book that was formative in your childhood – as potent as revisiting a lost place. The book's landscape is at once intimately known and unfamiliar; I seem to be stepping in the footprints I left when I was last here. Looking around with adult eyes, I suppose that I can see over the top of the wall of the secret garden: I can see the ideological underpinnings, understand the context, sniff out the falsities. And yet . . . submission is stronger. Or, at least, it is in the case of a book as richly, bravely, finely made as "The Secret

_Garden." My doubting, critical self seems smaller, moving around inside the novel's spaces, than the believing child who was here first. It's the adult who feels dwarfed and tiny within the huge shape of the child's experience.

(Hadley)

Here the gullible, submissive perspective of her childhood past is juxtaposed with the knowing, doubting perspective of her adult self. The conflict – "brave" versus "false", enchantment versus skepticism – is not just a conflict between two different ways of reading a story, of course; it is a conflict between an outlook that pervaded Hadley's childhood and an outlook that pervades her adulthood. As she rereads a childhood book, it is the childhood perspective that dominates; but the adult perspective remains. As she now lives her life, it is the adult perspective that dominates; but the childhood perspective is still present. Part of what is notable about Hadley's remarks is the respect that is granted to both perspectives, despite their conflict. The younger perspective does not alter the adult's life choices, and yet she gets to "keep" what happened, storing it and guarding it and "keeping faith" with it.[7]

To what extent do similar conflicts arise as we try to imagine our future self? Imagining, like remembering, might or might not evoke a first-person perspective; and it might evoke it to different degrees. I can imagine what it will be like to have my tooth pulled next week – imagining my head tilting backward, imagining the prick of a needle, imagining the dentist tugging on my jaw, and so on (this is the imagination counterpart of so-called episodic memory); or I can merely posit, and in that sense imagine, that I will have my tooth pulled next week (this is the counterpart of so-called semantic memory).[8] I can conjure up the anxiety I will feel in the dentist's office; or I can simply predict that I will be anxious. The accuracy with which we can anticipate a future experience from a first-person point of view will depend on a number of things: whether we have had similar experiences in the past, how good we are at spatial and emotional imagining, how much effort we are willing to devote to the task, and how much we know about the context of a future event. This is different from the case of memories, which often arrive unannounced, absent any effort and with minimal knowledge of the context; the first-person experience has already been stored, it does not need to be created – at least not to the same extent. We can suddenly remember sitting in a dentist's chair, for example, with no idea of when or where that was, and no explanation of why we remembered that now. The treacheries of memories, including first-person perspective memories, are well-known, however, and there is no reason to think that first-person memories, in general, are more accurate than first-person imaginings, in general.[9]

When we vividly imagine our future from a first-person point of view, and when we feel reasonably confident of the accuracy of that imagining, we experience an inner conflict that is much like the inner conflict of memory described before. The dental example is trivial but it illustrates the way that one's current stance on a future event (calm acceptance) can conflict with one's imagined future stance (anxiety). (In this example, the present outlook could just as well be the anxious one and the future outlook the calm one.) More significant inner conflicts can result from imagining a much slower and sadder future self, or a more confused and worried future self. To the extent that we believe that we are imagining our future accurately, and to the extent that that imagining is a regular part of our current experience, we may experience another case of double consciousness. As we shall see next, however, there is usually less reason to cultivate and sustain double consciousness regarding one's future than there is to sustain double consciousness regarding one's past.

## ENDING THE CONFLICT, OR NOT

In the case of remembering a past perspective and in the case of imagining a future perspective, certain ways of ending the conflict are not available to us. Unlike cases in which two parties to a quarrel might be able to resolve the conflict by one party conceding to the other, our conflicts with our past selves involve one party that cannot change because it no longer exists (my past self can't revise its outlook) and another that cannot really concede to the past because it can't go backwards in time and undo the changes that led from the earlier position to the later. The child that Hadley was can't abandon its gullible enthusiasm in favor of the mature cautiousness of her present self (which it probably couldn't understand anyway), and her present self can't regain a child's gullible enthusiasm (even if it wanted to). Similarly, though it is certainly possible for Hadley's present outlook to shift to a third option under the influence of her remembered past, this won't constitute a resolution (and won't end the inner conflict) without her past self changing as well; and that of course is not possible.[10]

Resolutions of conflicts with our imagined future selves may seem to hold more promise since those future selves don't yet exist, and we can shift from one imagined future to another. Perhaps my imagined future self should defer to my currently calm self (or, conversely, my currently calm self should defer to the anxiety of my imagined future self). In some cases, this seems right: not only possible, but advisable. In other important cases, though, it does not seem possible. If I imagine my future self as having significantly diminished mental abilities, for example, that future self will not really be in a position to concede to my present outlook (and my present self will not see any reason to concede to such a self); indeed, a mentally incapacitated self's indifference to various sorts of reasoning is what generates the conflict I now experience as I anticipate my likely future self.[11] Similarly, if I imagine my future self as increasingly disenchanted with the world due to its greater accumulation of disappointments and losses, it is hard to see how that future self could concede to my happier current self without its disappointments and losses being undone; and it is equally hard to see how my current self could concede to my future self's disenchantment without actually undergoing the relevant disappointments and losses.

There is a third type of resolution, however, that seems perfectly suited to conflicts between past and present, or present and future selves – namely, the subsumption of one view under, or within, another. (Hadley inverts the usual picture of a child's view contained within an adult's view when she says "It's the adult who feels dwarfed and tiny within the huge shape of the child's experience". But the containment imagery remains.) If we can view our past perspectives as somehow subsumed within our present perspective – as contributing to, rather than conflicting with, our present perspective (and, similarly, if we can view our present perspective as subsumed within our future perspective), then our inner conflicts concerning past and present might be resolved after all. Many biographies take this approach, portraying one's growth from a younger person to an older person as an accumulation of experiences that get integrated into an ever more complex perspective (whatever those experiences may be, and whatever that perspective may be).

There are many examples of this sort of progression in our lives: a childhood perception of love as feel-good bonding gets subsumed under an adult perception of love as openness and commitment; an early view of one's job as noble gets subsumed under a later view of it as high-minded but misguided; an initial impression of a social club as intolerant gets subsumed under one's subsequent understanding of them as anxious and self-protective. The later perspective places the earlier one in a larger context – a context that deepens and complicates one's thinking and one's responses, incorporating rather than rejecting the earlier perspective. But there are plenty of other examples where our lives don't proceed in this way, cases where a past point of view cannot be incorporated into one's present point of view: an earlier conception of romance may have little in common with one's later view; music that once seemed profound can now seem trite; the aspirations of a younger self may seem pointless to one's older self. (In each of these cases I am assuming the legitimacy of both views; one conflicts with the other without viewing the other as mistaken.) Our present outlook isn't simply an accumulation and a synthesis of past perspectives; sometimes it is an emphatic rejection of those perspectives.[12]

Sometimes, even the attempt to subsume one perspective under another seems like a case of bad faith – a clever attempt to evade responsibility for what one was or what one has become. Eliot's Balstrode, for example, tries to portray his confiscation of other people's property as a sophisticated way to serve his god:

> "Thou knowest how loose my soul sits from these things – how I view them all as implements for tilling Thy garden rescued here and there from the wilderness."

Metaphors and precedents were not wanting; peculiar spiritual experiences were not wanting which at last made the retention of his position seem a service demanded of him. . . . Balstrode's course up to that time had, he thought, been sanctioned by remarkable providences, appearing to point the way for him to be the agent in making the best use of a large property and withdrawing it from perversion.

(Eliot, chapter LXI)

Certainly, Balstrode would be more honest with himself if he could admit that he was once an exemplar of religious fervor and is now a defender of shady business practices. Similarly, when people try to subsume their theistic views under their scientific views by redefining "god" as "the origin of everything in the world" (i.e. the Big Bang?) or "that being greater than which nothing can be conceived", and redefining "will" as "whatever is causally efficacious", they seem unwilling to face up to the fact that they no longer believe in god or in free will.[13] Such redefinitions may preserve the acceptability of certain texts, or certain creeds, or certain practices that were meaningful in one's past, but they do so through trickery – effectively eliminating rather than subsuming the theism.

Compare these subsumption strategies to author Nancy Willard's embrace of magic and science:

I grew up aware of two ways of looking at the world that are opposed to each other and yet can exist side by side in the same person. One is the scientific view (my father was a scientist). The other is the magic view (my mother is a storyteller). Most of us come around at last to the scientific view. When we grow up, we put magic away with other childish things. But I think we can all remember a time when magic was as palatable as science, and the things we can't see were as important to us as the things we can.

. . . I believe that all small children and some adults hold this view at the same time that they hold the scientific one. I also believe that the great books for children come from those writers who hold both.

(Willard)

Willard does not redefine "magic" to mean *wondrous* so that science can subsume magic (or magic can subsume science); rather, she relishes a state of mind in which the magical view and the scientific view manage to coexist despite their evident opposition.[14]

It would be easy to end the conflict between magic and science by relegating magic to the domain of play, or the domain of children's books, allowing science full reign when it comes to our practical decisions, for example. Such separation is more difficult when it comes to conflicts between religion and science since religion as well as science is supposed to guide our practical decisions; but perhaps it is possible to wall off our ethical decisions (where religion is the authority) from our medical or mechanical decisions (where science is the authority). These are examples of what, in Chapter 1, we called separation solutions: they end a conflict by assigning separate domains to each side of the conflict. When it comes to remembered perspectives that conflict with present perspectives, might the sense of conflict be similarly eliminated by assigning separate *times* to each – remembered perspectives relegated to the past, present perspectives to the present?

There are several different ways in which this suggestion might be understood, some more plausible than others.

One way to relegate one's past perspectives to the past would be to stop remembering them – to stop bringing them into the present, where they don't belong. (Similarly, in the case of imagined futures, we might simply stop imagining our future selves.) This would require us to block their resurfacing in our lives – perhaps by a refusal to pay them any attention, perhaps by keeping ourselves engrossed in other things. The end result, however, would not be a case of separation so much as a case of dissolution: the conflict would disappear because one party to the conflict would simply disappear. Most of us would not want to forgo episodic memories of every past perspective that conflicts with our present outlook (nor to forgo vivid imagining of future outlooks), so even if this is a possible way to end inner conflict, it is not a desirable one.

Another way to relegate past perspectives to the past would be to treat them, when they do resurface, as the perspective of a self that no longer exists. Having episodic memories of a childhood sense of magic, or of a young adult's fervent belief in God, would be like visiting a virtual reality machine that has been programmed to recreate the experience of a certain child or a certain young adult at a distant time. One's present self could enjoy the first-person perspective of someone else but there would be no inner conflict if the other person's point of view was not experienced as one's own. But this is not the way that it feels; past outlooks, vividly recollected, still feel like a part of ourselves in a way that movie scenes, however vivid, do not. Perhaps we could learn to regard such recollections more like we regard virtual reality machines – as interesting opportunities to access the experiences of others. When the conflict concerns significant beliefs and values, however – beliefs and values that determine one's outlook on a wide range of things – the separation becomes harder. A virtual reality machine (or a powerful drug) that evoked a whole new way of looking at the world and our lives in it would not be so easily discounted as "some other person's view"; it would be more like being swept up in a movie whose outlook conflicts with our own – something that is bound to create an inner conflict, at least for a while.

It might be possible to regard each significant change in perspective – whether due to memory, or to a virtual reality machine, or to anything else – as a temporary change in self.[15] Galen Strawson defends both the possibility and the desirability of what he calls episodic selves – selves that last for relatively short times, disappearing (and being replaced with some other self) whenever there is a significant change of outlook. It is not clear just how short-lived a self can be in his account (he isn't in favor of long-term planning but he does think that episodic selves can be responsible selves). Strawson certainly allows for frequent changes from one self to another, however, and for regular oscillations between different selves. This introduces the possibility of treating the vivid resurfacing of a past perspective as the resurfacing of a past self. It is not clear why that self should have any quarrel with subsequent selves (they do not coexist in time), but even if a quarrel were to arise it would not be a quarrel with oneself. Clearly, this way of distinguishing selves is not the norm; but if it were sustainable (not just as a way of talking but as a way of living) it would be another way of avoiding inner conflict through effective separation.

Might the same separation be achieved through less radical means: by assigning past perspectives to a past *stage* of oneself (and future perspectives to a future stage of oneself)? The problem with this suggestion is that it either fails to end the conflict insofar as we experience the conflict between a past perspective and a present perspective (or a present perspective and a future perspective) as a conflict within ourselves now, or it becomes another version of Strawson's episodic selves. The conflict that interests us is, again, not one of logical contradiction (which is indeed avoided by distinguishing temporal stages) but one of experiential conflict – the experience of being pulled in two different directions at once.[16] One could, of course, turn to logic to help alleviate the sense of inner conflict. *Reexperiencing* a past perspective from the first-person point of view is not the same as now *adopting* that perspective any more than imagining is believing; even if the look and feel of the two experiences were identical, they are framed and aimed in different ways.[17] But this underestimates the disruptive power of the way things now look and feel, and it overestimates the calming power of logic; or, put another way, it overestimates the "cure" that can be effected through linguistic analysis.[18] When I am vividly experiencing a conflict between conflicting points of view, I can't discount the pull of my past self simply by reminding myself that I am merely remembering and not now endorsing.

Cora Diamond makes a still stronger claim, insisting that the attempt to overcome conflict through linguistic analysis (and, more particularly, through the differentiation of language games) often functions to deflect us from the deeper difficulties of our lives and our world. Describing someone's bewilderment that someone now dead could appear so live in a photograph, she writes:

> Now it is plainly possible to describe the photo so it does not seem boggling at all. It is a photo of men who

died young, not long after the picture was taken. Where is the contradiction? Taking the picture that way, there is no problem about our concepts being adequate to describe it. Again, one might think of how one would teach a child who had been shown a photo and told it was a photo of her grandfather, whom she knows to be dead. If she asks "Why is he smiling if he's dead?", she might be told that he was smiling when the picture was taken, because he was not dead then, and that he died later. The child is being taught the language-game, being shown how her problem disappears as she comes to see how things are spoken of in the game. The point of view from which she sees a problem is not yet in the game; while that from which the horrible contradiction impresses itself on the poet-speaker is that of someone who can no longer speak within the game.

(Diamond 2)[19]

Diamond wants to do justice to the impression of a "horrible contradiction" – even (perhaps especially) if the contradiction disappears once we enter into standard language games. We miss out on something important if we treat profound disruptions in our sense of the world as nothing more than confusions about the proper use of ordinary language.

## NARRATED SELVES AND FOLDED SELVES

We have been focusing on memories that are relived from the first-person point of view (so-called "episodic" memories) as opposed to memories that are merely recounted (so-called "semantic" memories). It is common, of course, for our relived memories to be replaced by recounted memories (you remember that you once believed in god, but you no longer remember what it was like) – in which case no experience of conflict from the first-person point of view remains. It is also common for our relived memories to be transformed in ways that mitigate the sense of conflict with our present perspectives. In many cases the past experience comes back to us in a watered-down, washed-out form – no longer so poignant, no longer so detailed – and there is very little sense of conflict as a result. Such depletion often happens automatically and is not under our control. In other cases, past experiences are relived in a highly-selective, stylized form – designed to buttress overly-idealistic views of our ourselves, for example – and, again, the conflict between past and present perspectives tends to disappear. Nicholas Dames uses the term "nostalgic memory" to describe memory that selects those aspects of the past that best cohere with one's overall sense of what life should be (from one's present point of view).[20] Dames notes that the path that leads us from one memory to another, i.e. associative memory, is guided by principles of relevance, concordance, and integrity. The mind gravitates towards memories that reinforce a unified view of oneself and one's past, avoiding memories that are disruptive of that view.

> Each principle is describing not only the normal conditions of remembrance but its optimal conditions, and both the normative and the ideal cohere in a vision of a mind that can tell a highly organized and pruned version of the past, one with the proper narrative virtues of cause and effect, an economy of detail, and a concatenation of prolepses and informative analepses [i.e. flashes forward and flashes backward].
>
> (Dames 134)

A similar selectiveness in favor of unity governs the way we imagine our future. I imagine my future self as an extension of my present self – changing, of course, but changing in directions I am already headed in (for better or for worse), and changing for reasons that make perfectly good sense from my current point of view. Imagining myself with a poor memory, for example, makes sense as an extension from current failures of memory, and imagining a future acceptance of death makes sense in light of the increasing number of deaths that surround older people. Imagining a radically different future self may be more difficult than remembering a radically different past self, however, insofar as our present self puts more constraints on our projected self than on our remembered self. While I can vividly recall what it was like to have a radically different outlook on religion, or on music, for example, it is hard for me to vividly imagine yet another outlook on those things that is equally foreign to my present self – the outlook of a jihadist, for example, or the experience of someone who is tone deaf. So, while we may be able to resist the unifying distortions of memory, we may not be able to resist the unifying distortions of imagining.

Sometimes the felt conflict between past and present perspectives is elusive – a lingering sense of unease with respect to the past rather than a clear confrontation with some vividly remembered experience (or some vividly imagined future). People revisiting a childhood home, school, or town are frequently disconcerted by the contrast between their first-person memories and their first-person experiences of a place – without being able to say just what it is that has changed. Years later these places can look different to us even if little has changed, largely because our own outlook has changed; and the evident disparity can lead us to view our past selves in a different light as well (as more vulnerable, more narcissistic, or more anxious, for example). Similarly, reconnecting with old friends can create the uncanny sense that we are encountering a different person in the same body – an experience that might reveal more about changes in ourselves than in them.

The inner divide that results from combining past and present perspectives might be temporary or it might be lasting. Anita Brookner presents us with a character Hertz, who seems permanently unsettled by the mismatch between his past attachments and his present sense of alienation from those attachments. Repeatedly reviewing old photographs,

> He felt a distaste, but also a curiosity that always accompanied this particular investigation: the photographs, of no conceivable relevance to anyone he currently knew, were to him a painful record of people whose hold on his affections had dwindled to almost nothing.
>
> (Brookner 116)

He is quite conscious of the contrast between his past and his present perspective, and he is perpetually preoccupied by it. Hertz's preoccupation with the contrast between present and past is not very appealing; he seems like a sad character, not an admirable one. Why, then, should any of us continue to conjure up perspectives from our past? An occasional dip into the past may be interesting, and instructive, but living always haunted by one's past can seem downright dysfunctional.

There is a sense in which we can't put our past behind us without keeping it alive. A consciously recalled experience registers as a memory in a way that unconscious influences from the past do not. When I consciously recall a particular experience of my mother and the way it made me feel, I recognize it as a memory; it is not the scene now before my eyes, and it is not my mother as I now know her. These distinctions disappear when memories are unconscious. Many experiences from our childhood continue to influence the way we feel and the way we perceive the world around us, and some of those childhood feelings (e.g. fear, glee, loneliness) and some of those childhood perceptions (of danger, of opportunity, of abandonment) can be unconsciously reactivated when we meet people similar to those we knew in childhood, or when we are in situations similar to those we encountered as a child.[21] As long as these memories remain unconscious, however, we will not be able to separate them off from our present feelings and perceptions; we will have no ability to distinguish past influences from present influences, and we will have no way to limit the influence of our memories. Keeping the distinction between past and present clearly in mind enables us to perceive things more accurately (an epistemic advantage) and it enables us to act more effectively (a practical advantage). Indeed, one of the oft-cited purposes of therapies that get us to recall past experiences – to bring them into consciousness as memories – is to enable us to distinguish past from present and, thereby, to gain some degree of control over the influence of our past.[22] Rather than seeping unawares into our present outlook, a conscious recollection of the past is able to retain its distinctness from the present. As a result, we are better at either resolving or tolerating or even relishing inner conflicts – because we are better at distinguishing the sources and the characters of competing perspectives.

Conscious recollection and recognized separation of past from present is not only important for knowledge (as it helps us to retain truer versions of both past and future), or for smooth functioning in the world (as it helps us to defend ourselves against inappropriate incursions from the past). Episodic memory also has a "metaphysical" significance insofar as it adds an extra "dimension" to our lives. Consider the following passage from Francoise Melzer's meditations on memory:

> The effort to retain a remembered image by an act of will remains, as before; but now there is also the capacity to see in the fading light of the present-as-place the unchanging luminosity of memory itself as that which both gives back the vision of a vanished past and simultaneously keeps it within the confines of that which cannot be recaptured. Existence is "augmented," more profound, perhaps because when the dimension of the past opens up as an icon of memory to be contemplated, the present-as-place is deepened by the added dimension, vibrating between two places.
>
> (Meltzer 233)

In this description, our ongoing access to a past point of view (that is recognized as past) effectively "deepens" our lives by creating an extra "place" in the present – a place that must be located "behind" the place we now live in. The added "place" of ongoing memory might also be described as an "inner space" – a space that is no longer a part of external reality. Thus the image of an added "dimension".

"Folding" is another metaphor for combining past and present without erasing their distinctness. Deleuze introduced this image in his book on Foucault (1988), and later elaborated in his book on Leibniz and the Baroque (1992). If we imagine a timeline, along which events in the world arrange themselves in a single dimension, folding is the process through which past points along the line are brought into the present – the presently experienced, that is – which, in Deleuze's words, is also the process by which the outside becomes inside, and the process by which inner "space" is created. "[W]e follow the folds, reinforce the doublings from snag to snag, and surround ourselves with foldings that form an 'absolute memory', in order to make the outside into a vital, recurring element" (*The Fold* 2). *? what?*

Deleuze notes the importance of "snags" to secure the doublings that create folds. Snags are points that stop a fabric (here, the fabric of space and time) from flowing smoothly. What creates a snag in this case is a misfit, or a conflict, between a remembered past and an experienced present. Left to the unconscious, such conflicts tend to disappear into a smoother whole – an unreflective blend of past and present; and, in any case, the contours of our unconscious mind will not be experienced as the contours of an "inner" life. Put another way, the experience of an inner life, or inner "space", depends on a contrast between inner and outer life, and the unconscious is not able to make that distinction. With consciousness, we are able to distinguish between things that are presently perceived and things that are merely remembered (or imagined) – a contrast that is prompted by various conflicts in our experience. Apparent contradictions in the outer world can be reconfigured as inner conflicts – between past and present, between remembered and perceived. Far from resolving these conflicts (which no longer have the status of contradictions), they are preserved in our inner lives, contributing to the "spaciousness" of that dimension of our lives.

I want to mention two other benefits that come with a sustained awareness of past versus present perspectives. *First,* continued awareness of a past perspective makes us sharply aware of the changeability of our outlook. It is one thing to know in a general sort of way that we have changed, or to be occasionally reminded of a specific change; it is another thing to live with the contrast as a more constant presence. When we continue to compare our present perspective to a different perspective from our past, it is harder to ignore the downsides of our present perspective, and it is harder to forget its precariousness. (The same could be said for continuing to compare our current perspective with the perspective of people from the past; but these comparisons will not have the affective force of our episodic memories.) Second, ongoing awareness of a past perspective can add to our sense of responsibility for the choices and the actions that resulted from that perspective. In most cases, the choices and the actions of our past were not isolated events, they were expressions of whatever outlook we had at the time. Conjuring up that past reminds us of how deep-going our involvement was in the choices and actions of our past, which encourages us to take greater responsibility for those choices and actions; and the more persistent our recall of a past perspective, the more persistent our sense of responsibility for the choices and actions of that past time.[23]

## THREE MODELS, APPLIED

Chapter 1 offered three models for the continuation of double consciousness: juggling, isometrics, and disruption. How might each of these models be applied to cases of temporal doubling?

In some respects, juggling past and present outlooks (or present and future outlooks) is exactly like juggling different outlooks in the present – the outlook of a Mexican versus the outlook of an American, the outlook of a woman versus the outlook of a man, the outlook of a theist versus the outlook of a scientist, and so on. For, as we have seen, episodic memory (or imaginative anticipation) can reactivate a past perspective (or pre-activate a future perspective), creating a conflict within one's current experience. We can entertain both of these competing perspectives at once – alert to their respective insights – without feeling the need for any sort of resolution. When we juggle the contrasting perspectives, we attempt to keep each "afloat", allowing them to play off each other. We recall the way a certain piece of music (or a certain kind of chatter) used to affect us, noting the contrast with our current response and we keep both in mind as we continue to listen.

*both views*

There is a subtle difference, however, between juggling conflicting perspectives from the present and juggling conflicting perspectives from the past. When we relive a past perspective on some object or situation, we *know that* the object or situation of that past outlook is the same as the object or situation we are presently attending to, but we may not *experience* the two objects or situations as the same one. Vividly recalling our past enjoyment of (or boredom with) a certain piece of music, for example, need not interfere with our current boredom with (or enjoyment of) that music; for, I am suggesting, we can realize that the two responses – both present within our current experience – were prompted by the same piece without, however, experiencing them both as responses to this piece. Similarly, episodic memories of our past impatience with (or delight in) young children will conflict with our current delight in (or impatience with) young children, but they need not interfere with our present perceptions; for, again, we can know that it was precisely the same behavior that prompted the past response (now retrieved in memory) without experiencing both responses as responses to the behavior now before us. In many cases, we are not even capable

**Temporal Doubling**

*79*

of experiencing the two responses as responses to the same thing. We might recall how Black Sabbath sounded to us in the past but the connection between that experience and our present experience of the same music is purely intellectual; we know that they are competing responses to the same music but we can't experience them as such (we can't affect this kind of gestalt switch in the present). This doesn't prevent us from juggling back and forth between our memories and our present perceptions ("Children used to seem like that, but now they seem like this"), and from noticing the conflict between their respective outlooks, but it may mean that we know without being able to experience the fact that they are alternate perspectives on the very same things.

Juggling current and future perspectives also requires us to conjure up an outlook from another time (and to continue to juxtapose that outlook with our present outlook) without necessarily engaging in a series of gestalt switches with regard to the scene before us. Suppose one is able to conjure up a future point of view according to which one's current decision not to have children seems selfish, short-sighted, even tragic. And suppose that point of view conflicts with one's present point of view according to which the decision not to have children seems realistic, responsible, even courageous. Also common is the contrast between once finding the prospect of children desirable and later finding it undesirable (Donath). There is validity to both points of view, and there is no middle position that would allow one to have it both ways. While one must make a decision one way or another, it is perfectly possible (and, I would argue, often desirable)[24] to continue to keep both perspectives in mind – recognizing the clash of perspectives, recognizing the necessary trade-off between present and future perspectives. Nonetheless, it is likely that imagining a future perspective from which the decision not to have children seem mistaken will not affect how the prospect of children looks and feels now.

The isometrics model offers a more confrontational way of combining past and present (or present and future) perspectives. Isometric exercises work by intensifying an opposition, pushing or pulling in opposite directions in order to strengthen the relevant muscles and in order to increase one's overall stability. Applied to the case of past versus present perspectives, the isometrics model recommends an intentional intensification of the opposition. Recall (from before) how Hadley reread a story from her childhood and her old susceptibility to enchantment was reawakened. The contrast between her past submission to magic and the critical scrutiny of her present brings both into sharper relief, and though she describes the reawakened submissiveness as now "dwarfing" the adult scrutiny, it is clear that the strength of each outlook actually adds to the strength of the other. The childhood story becomes even more enchanting against the backdrop of the adult's doubts, and the adult's doubts become even more pointed against the backdrop of the child's enchantment; the story would be less seductive if it were thought to be realistic (not an occasion for doubt) and one's doubts would have less bite if the story were less compelling (not an occasion for enchantment). This particular contrast – between susceptibility and doubt, between submission and criticism – is familiar from many contexts outside of our (re)reading of fairy tales, of course. Many people recall a gullible enthusiasm from the past that conflicts with their present mature cautiousness towards almost everything – towards upcoming trips, ongoing projects, new friendships, major purchases, and so on. Insofar as we honor both perspectives (neither one being more "correct" than the other) and keep both in mind, this produces a significant and lasting instance of inner conflict. The isometrics model for sustaining this inner conflict (this form of double consciousness) encourages us to "lean into" both – cultivating each, relishing their respective merits, deepening their hold on us – with the expectation that both perspectives will be strengthened rather than weakened by intensifying the conflict in this way.

In addition to strengthening opposing forces by intensifying their opposition, following the isometrics model can improve one's overall balance and stability – psychological balance and psychological stability in this case. Past aspects of ourselves, including past ways of perceiving and understanding the world around us, tend to hang around, whether recognized or not. The perceptual and conceptual tendencies we had as children may not be apparent in the present but they usually remain as latent dispositions – tendencies that, in the right circumstances, can and will be reactivated. Bringing those tendencies to light and giving them a larger role in our current life can contribute to our psychological balance and stability – both because we won't be surprised by their power over us if they are in plain view and because they can counterbalance (and be counterbalanced by) competing parts of ourselves.[25] In the previously cited passage from Proust, Marcel's current discouragement and anxiety is countered by vivid recollections of a past happiness and calm. Those recollections serve to stabilize his current mood by evoking its opposite, and even if he isn't able to view his current situation from the same happy point of view, the very fact that that point of view has reappeared makes it more likely that it will be active in the future.

Our third model for the continuation of double consciousness was the model of disruption – an approach whereby

**Why It's OK** to Be of Two Minds

dominant perceptions and dominant schemas are deliberately disrupted by the promotion of their opposites (or, if not their opposites, their contraries). Assuming that the dominant schema is one's present schema, one might search one's past for disruptive alternatives and one might seek to re-experience those alternatives as a way to fuel one's advocacy of an alternative. It is possible to read the progression of Balstrode's views in this way. His earlier life was dominated by a righteous outlook that came to seem too simple-minded and constraining; he effectively displaced that outlook with a more worldly and accommodating point of view (for which he offered detailed and imaginative defenses) – until it began to feel too easy and too empty; then, and only then, he conjured up the past perspective that was most capable of condemning his present perspective.[26] It is also possible to read some imaginative forays into the future in this way. If your present outlook is carefree, try to conjure up a future without any safety net; but if your present outlook is extremely conscientious, try to conjure up a future in which you die young. If your present outlook is trusting, imagine a future of betrayals; but if your present outlook is distrustful, try to imagine a future without any close relationships. Whether one looks to the past or to the future to find suitable disruptors, the aim is to counteract the complacency and stagnation that comes from acceding to the dominant view (whatever that view may be).

Different models may be suitable for different circumstances or for different people. Being a creative provocateur (following the disrupter model) may be especially relevant in cases where the dominant outlooks feels especially suffocating or boring – which may be the case for some but not all; and some people may be more adept at (or take more pleasure in) conjuring up clever alternatives from the past or future. Practicing mental isometrics, on the other hand, may be especially relevant in cases where people are haunted (whether happily or unhappily) by their pasts; and some people are better than others at strengthening their memories or at leaning into a conflict. For most people in most cases of temporal doubling, the juggling model will be the easiest to follow; but successful juggling depends on a kind of agility and continual alertness that may not suit all people or all situations.

## CLOSING REMARKS ON THE PERCEPTION OF TIME

Much has been written on the subjective experience of time – on when and how time seems to speed up, or slow down, or to stand still, for example. Most of this research looks for correlations between different sorts of activities and different senses of time, or between different types of attention and different senses of time.[27] I expect that there are also some interesting correlations between different sorts of remembering and different senses of time. I would expect episodic remembering (reliving a past episode from a first-person point of view) to correlate with a less linear and less smooth sense of time than the sense of time that is correlated with remembering an event semantically, as part of one's self-narrative. And because episodic remembering is more saturated remembering – more senses activated, more details to attend to – I would expect episodic remembering to be correlated with a sense of time passing more slowly.

When episodic remembering is more or less constant, as in the cases we have been describing in this chapter, there are several possible effects on our sense of time. On the one hand, the steady memory of a past outlook (or the steady anticipation of a future outlook) within one's present experience might produce a sense of block time, with all events equally real at any given time – thus a sense of time as having come to a halt. On the other hand, the steady awareness of significant conflicts between past and present might heighten one's sense of temporal contrasts – making time seem to pass more quickly. Different styles of sustaining double consciousness regarding our pasts might also have different effects on our sense of time. An isometrics approach, by strengthening the stability of our experience, might also produce a sense of time as something more permanent; whereas a disruptive approach, by continually dislodging the currently dominant view, might produce a sense of time as fragile and fleeting.

These reflections are merely speculative, of course. It is not clear how they could be tested. But they do suggest that the way we experience our pasts could have an effect on the way we experience time itself.

# Three

> His desires remained memorized within her. She looked at the attractive women he would look at. . . . She appraised their eyes and mouths and wondered about their bodies. She had become him. She longed for these women. But she was also herself and so she despised them. She lusted after them but she also wanted to beat them up.
>
> (Moore 33)

This passage comes from a short story by Lorrie Moore, entitled "Community Life", about ways that we allow or don't allow others to enter into our lives. Often, when someone matters enough to us, we carry their point of view alongside our own – creating a distinctive sort of double consciousness. Unlike the cases of double consciousness described in Chapters 1 and 2, where the conflict exists between different aspects of oneself or different stages of oneself, here the conflict is between oneself and an internalized Other. While conflicts resulting from an internalized Other can be problematic in any number of ways, I hope to show that in many cases the resulting double consciousness ought to be retained rather than resisted or resolved.

## INTERNALIZED OTHERS

When we internalize other people, we remain aware of their views (or what we take to be their views) even when they are absent. Theirs becomes a lens through which we perceive the world around us even as we continue to perceive things in our own, different way. In the passage quoted prior, the character Olena takes on the lustful outlook of her boyfriend Nick without abandoning her own dislike of the women she views as threats. There is a clear conflict between the two perspectives: attraction and repulsion pull in opposite directions. Yet she continues to occupy both perspectives on the women she observes. This short story does not tell us how long this inner conflict continues, and it does not tell us whether Olena has also internalized other aspects of Nick's outlook. So her state of mind may or may not qualify as a state of double consciousness as we have defined it, where the conflict must be significant and lasting. But it is not hard to find cases where these requirements are met.

Many of us have internalized the views of a parent or a religion or a teacher in such a way that we remain aware of their way of approaching the world long past the time we are exposed to them. We encounter a new person or a new situation and we immediately recognize that person or that situation as one that our mother would view as "welcoming" (or as "unwelcoming") for example. And that word evokes an entire schema of associations and valuations that came with our mother's use of that term. We consider what we want (or don't want) for our children and an internalized religious schema points us towards possibilities that are "worthy" or "righteous" or "blessed" (versus "unworthy", "wicked", or "cursed"). We listen to an economist or a politician through the schema of a

**Why It's OK** to Be of Two Minds

favorite professor who would have viewed them as defenders of "the panopticon" or "purveyors of surveillance capitalism". These are not isolated incidents for we often encounter new people and situations, we often think of what we want for our children, and we are often faced with people who are attempting to control other people. Nor, cumulatively anyway, are they insignificant. But do they produce the inner conflict needed for double consciousness?

In some cases there is no inner conflict because one never manages to distinguish one's own views from the views of the other person – as a child might fail to distinguish her views from those of her mother.[1] Or there might be no inner conflict because one always defers to the views of the other – as a devotee might always defer to his guru. One has never gained independence from the other person or one has lost it; the internalized Other has become oneself, and there is no conflict to contend with. We imagine our mother's voice describing a home as "welcoming" but it could just as well be our own voice. We recall our professor describing certain public policies as creating "a panopticon" or supporting "surveillance capitalism", but this is the way we now think of them as well.

In other cases, there is no inner conflict because the perspective of a remembered or imagined Other was never really internalized. I might regularly recall the outlook of an eccentric neighbor, for example, without ever "taking it to heart"; or I might continue to imagine the views of an outspoken politician without those views having any grip on me.[2] Here the lack of inner conflict is not a matter of failing to imagine the other's point of view "from the inside" or in sufficient detail; it is, rather, a matter of the relevant imagining never becoming automatic or second nature. I may think of my eccentric neighbor often and imagine his take on a recent event; but my mother's response comes to me unbidden, whether I am actively thinking of her or not. The religious schema that she uses to organize her experience is frequently activated alongside my own non-religious schema, without any effort on my part. Or, in the case of an influential teacher, his critical take on the news unfolds more or less automatically alongside my own, different take on that same news.

There is a subtle but important difference between the sorts of double consciousness described in Chapter 1, where the conflicting schemas characterize different sides of oneself, and the sort of double consciousness addressed here, where the conflict is between one's own schema and that of an internalized Other. In this latter type of double consciousness, we *identify* with one view and not with the other – even as we continue to view the world through the lenses of both schemas. We see the world through the eyes of someone else but we refuse to *own* that view. What does it mean to identify with a view, or to take it as one's own? It involves such things as explicitly endorsing that view, being willing to act on it, and taking responsibility for its implications. (More precisely, identifying with a view requires us to be *disposed* to endorse it, to act on it, and to take responsibility for it. Circumstances won't always allow one to manifest these dispositions.) The view of an internalized Other might be rejected outright ("I think her view is wrong") or it may simply be disowned ("That's not my view"); either way, it is registered as an outlook that is "not mine".[3]

Registering a view as "not mine" is not enough to prevent a state of inner conflict, however. In Chapter 2 we noted how first-person memories of a past outlook – an outlook that one no longer endorses or acts upon, can make that past outlook return in ways that generate an experiential conflict. I might now regard my past outlook as overly trusting and blinkered, but vividly recalling that outlook can make my present outlook seem overly cautious and closed-minded, and the juxtaposition of these two perspectives can make me feel conflicted – even as I continue to endorse and to act on my current perspective. Likewise, the perspective of an internalized Other can exist alongside the perspective I call my own and can result in a conflict between two different ways of schematizing the information I receive from the world. We can be "moved" by views that we "disown", where its "pull" on us can create an inner *?* conflict despite our clear rejection of that view. *what*

This phenomenon is familiar but can be clarified through a consideration of competing dispositions. As is frequently noted, the viewpoint one is disposed to voice or to publicly endorse can differ from the viewpoint one is disposed to act on; we say that we are sympathetic but our actions are unsympathetic, we explicitly endorse a particular set of rules but we act to undermine them.[4] Less frequently noted is the way that the views we are disposed to endorse and to act on can differ from the views that govern much of our thinking, our feeling, and our imagining. We might find ourselves constantly thinking about how our mother or our teacher would view our situation – without ever endorsing their views; we might find ourselves feeling some of what they would feel in our situation – without ever acting on the basis of these feelings; and we might find ourselves imagining the outcomes that they would imagine – without allowing those imaginings to enter into our own planning. There is no self-deception in these cases as we are perfectly aware of the mismatch between our own views and the views of the internalized Other, and we neither speak nor act on the basis of the latter. Thoughts and feelings and

imaginings each activate their own dispositions, however –
dispositions to follow some trains of thought rather than others, dispositions to respond in some ways rather than others,
and dispositions to see things some ways rather than others.
So the ongoing presence of alien thoughts, feelings, and imaginings whose contents conflict with the contents of our own
beliefs, values, and perceptions will create an inner conflict
insofar as we must make an effort to discount a habitual way
of thinking, to discredit feelings that have become automatic,
and to bracket off imagining that is misleading. There is no *logical* conflict between thinking one thing and believing another,
between feeling one thing and valuing another, or between
imagining one thing and perceiving another; but, at least when
these contrasts are ongoing, there is a *psychological* conflict.

The extent of the psychological conflict will depend, of
course, on how different the internalized outlook is and how
pervasive it is. The psychological conflict created by the internalization of a religious view that one adamantly rejects will
be greater than the conflict created by the internalization of
a teacher with views that are only slightly to the left of one's
own. Views that diverge with respect to all social relations will
generate more conflict than views that diverge merely with
respect to the raising of children. Also, some views may be
more deeply internalized than others – eliciting deeper feelings
and more extensive imagining – and that too will increase the
inner conflict.

### EMPATHIZING WITH OTHERS

What is the difference between internalizing someone else's
point of view and empathizing with someone else's point of
view? In both cases we imagine how things appear to that

person and we recognize that our own view of things may be quite different. The perspective of an internalized Other is one that we carry with us always, however, and it is automatically triggered by any number of situations that we encounter in daily life. My mother's religious outlook, for example, often occurs to me unbidden when I write a letter, plan a trip, or interact with a child. Empathizing with another person, on the other hand, happens when that other person is explicitly considered and usually requires more effort.[5] I try to imagine how the receiver of my letter will view my news, how a fellow traveler will respond to a particular scene, or how my remarks must sound to the child I am speaking with. Habitual empathy towards another person (a close friend for example) can evolve into the internalization of that person if their outlook starts occurring to us automatically and effortlessly; conversely, it can sometimes take an effort to imagine the perspective of someone we have internalized (our mother, for example). So there are some interesting in-between cases, but the basic distinction between automatic versus deliberate imagining of another person's perspective remains useful.

Empathy, if sufficiently rich in detail and in feeling, can create a state of inner conflict. Empathizing with a friend's pessimism can create an inner struggle with one's own optimism, for example, and empathy with a companion's fear can compete with one's own confidence. Some people are better than others at maintaining a barrier between the states with which they empathize and the states they consider their own, but it does not seem possible to empathize fully with a competing view without feeling one's own view challenged by it. Still, our efforts at empathy are usually limited in both scope and time (we tend to imagine a small bit of the other's experience then quickly return to our own outlook and preoccupations), so the inner conflicts generated by empathy are usually too shallow and too fleeting to give rise to a double consciousness (where, as explained in Chapter 1, the conflict must be significant and lasting).

There are at least two kinds of cases, however, where empathy and its attendant conflicts can be significant and lasting. First, there are cases where one devotes a significant part of one's time trying to empathize with a particular person or group – without, however, coming to know them in the automatic way that would count as internalization. It can be like this for parents, for spouses, for therapists, or for anthropologists, for example. The parent of an autistic child may struggle to empathize with her child's outlook on the world, and the imagining that requires may be extensive and lasting without ever becoming automatic. Similarly, a therapist may work hard to empathize with a distressed client, or an anthropologist may spend long stretches of time trying to imagine the perspective of people from another culture. Those who live with animals or study animals may also spend a lot of time trying to imagine the alternate perspective of non-human animals. In each of these examples, a large part of one's mental "space" will be taken up with the attempt to imagine a very different way of experiencing the world – so that one's imagining of the other's experience, though it continues to be effortful, becomes a constant in one's own life. In these cases, when there is an inner conflict it will be lasting, and the outcome may indeed be a state of double consciousness.

A second case of lasting empathy occurs when people are constantly imagining the views of those around them in order to maneuver more successfully in their social situation. This might not be the best strategy for social success – both because one's imagining is often mistaken and because there are usually more straightforward strategies for advancing one's interests. But imagining the views of those around us is certainly a common preoccupation and for some it is nearly constant. Many teenagers, for example, obsess over the views of their peers, perpetually imagining what their peers think about a joke, an outfit, a friend, whatever. And the same obsession can be found in adults who are particularly worried (for good reason or bad) about how the views of others might diverge from their own. I am not thinking of cases like that described by Du Bois where a dominant social view is internalized to create one side of one's double consciousness (though this can, of course, happen with teens in their social milieu); I am thinking instead of cases where imagining others' points of view continues to be a project rather than automatic. When that imagining sets up an ongoing conflict in one's own thinking and feeling – a conflict between thinking certain behavior is appropriate and thinking it is not, between thinking certain people are admirable and thinking they are not, between feeling proud and pleased and feeling disgusted, and so on – the conditions for double consciousness will be met.

## LOVING AND BEING IN LOVE

When we love someone, we tend to spend a lot of time imagining their point of view, which can provide us with an alternate perspective on the world around us. This imagining may be automatic – because of our internalization of that person, or it may be more deliberate – because of our intentional empathy with that person. In either case, if there are significant and lasting differences between the perspectives of the lover and the loved, the result will be another familiar form of double consciousness.

Being in love involves something more. Many accounts of erotic love claim that a lover desires to merge with the beloved, and many defenders of such accounts understand this desire for merger as a kind of reversion to the state of an infant or a young child for which the line between inner and outer, between me and you, disappears. Aristophanes's speech, in Plato's *Symposium* on (erotic) love, described love as the desire to rejoin a lost half of oneself, to return to one's original, not-yet-split-off state of being.[6] Freud (*Civilization and its Discontents*) understood the draw of love as the temptation to regress to an earlier, less-conflicted relation to another.[7] Sartre characterizes erotic love as a desire to erase the boundaries between self and other by possessing and subsuming that other within oneself.[8] Edith Spector Person describes the lover's desire for merger as follows:

> [T]he lover seeks to dissolve the barrier between the self and the beloved. Since the barrier is the self's boundary, what is sought is a form of self-transcendence. Thus there is a striking overlap between the language of love and that of religion, particularly that of religious mysticism. Some degree of self-surrender in the service of self-purification and self-transformation is a necessary component of merger, of those epiphanies intrinsic to passionate love.
>
> (137)

There are many reasons to think that such a merger is not possible – or, at best, that it is possible for very brief periods with respect to very limited parts of ourselves. A merger of sexual desires, for example, is restricted in both duration and scope. (There is, moreover, a serious instability in the very desire to merge with an Other since successful merger would entail the elimination of otherness. Put another way, the satisfaction of one's desire to merge with another would also be the end of erotic love insofar as there would no longer be an independent object of desire.) Being "in love", then, might be construed as a largely ill-fated attempt to overcome the double consciousness that comes with an intense and sustained awareness of the otherness of another person; one seeks either to absorb the other into oneself or to be absorbed by the other. This is the clearly doomed state of Olena in the passage that opens this chapter: she makes her lover's desires into her own ("She had become him") only to recoil at the realization that those desires work against her own. Abandoning the attempt at merger, however, means no longer being in love – even as it may also facilitate more successful loving of the other person.

It is tempting to think that we can internalize others or continue to empathize with others without generating a state of inner conflict. The available cures are often worse than the disease, however. In Chapter 1 we canvassed three distinct ways of overcoming perspectival conflict – resolution, separation, and dissolution. How do each of these options fare with respect to the double consciousness that can come with internalization or with sustained empathy?

## POSSIBLE RESOLUTIONS

Conflict resolutions, as described in Chapter 1, include concessions, compromises, and subsumptions. In the case of an internalized Other, where another person's outlook is automatically imagined but still recognized as an outlook that is not one's own, it is not usually possible for the actual other to concede to one's own point of view (usually they are not around and may not even be aware of one's own point of view). We can imagine concessions on the part of the internalized Other, of course – I could imagine my mother, for example, conceding that there is not in fact a god – but such imagining is unlikely to change the internalized version of that person, the version that is called up automatically. Furthermore, in most cases, we want the views of others who have mattered to us to stay with us even when (and perhaps especially when) recalling their views causes discomfort.[9] Concessions *to* the internalized Other are even more problematic insofar as they forgo one's own independence from the other for the sake of internal harmony. And compromise (if it were possible) would involve both of these losses – loss of one's automatic access to the original other and loss of one's own independence from that other.

Subsumptions, on the other hand, are undesirable insofar as they tend to diminish both the subsumed and the subsuming points of view. I could try to subsume an internalized religious perspective within my atheism by adopting it as a reassuring fiction; but that would diminish both the power of the religious outlook and the power of my atheism. Or I could try to subsume my atheism under an internalized religious outlook by regarding it as part of God's plan for me; but, again, that would detract from the force of my atheism (presenting it as a personal challenge rather than a metaphysical truth) and it would detract from the force of the religious view I have internalized (making God into someone who chooses to delude people). I would rather continue to experience both views richly and automatically, feeling the conflict but knowing that one is the view of my internalized mother and the other mine. Holding onto this sort of double consciousness does not give both perspectives equal power over me (I recognize my mother's view

**Why It's OK** to Be of Two Minds

as hers, not mine, and I act on mine, not hers), and it does not stop me from believing that her religious beliefs are mistaken; but it allows me to continue to experience my mother's outlook from the inside while adhering to my own very different point of view.

Unlike the case of an internalized Other, the person with whom we empathize is often present and able to participate in a resolution; talking things through we might arrive at a shared outlook. Furthermore, our imagining of their point of view does not occur automatically, so it is easier to alter our imagining of their viewpoint if a resolution can be found. But the same worries about losing one's independence and losing some of the distinctive insights of each perspective, remain. Many real-life attempts at concession or compromise involve some degree of some form of coercion, whether or not this is recognized by the participants. And many subsumptions (whether effected in conversation or in one's imagination) end up disempowering at least one of the views involved. (The religion versus atheism example elaborated prior works just as well when the other is someone we empathize with rather than someone whom we have internalized.) This does not mean that conversation should be avoided, but it does mean that conversations with others ought to have the aim of fuller understanding of that other rather than the resolution of differences.

Might love be different? Might love be a case where the autonomy of the relevant parties ought to be sacrificed for the harmony offered by some sort of resolution? At least one tradition understands marriage as an arrangement whereby "two shall become one", whether that be through concession, compromise, or subsumption (typically, subsumption of a woman under a man); and it is certainly possible for people to aspire to such a union. Not everyone values autonomy above all else and not everyone is concerned with the power imbalances that might bring about such a union. Indeed, as indicated previously, there is reason to think that erotic love, or the state of being in love, is a state of desiring such a union (however irrational and however unconscious that desire may be). Putting aside the obvious worries about power imbalances and lost autonomy, though, it is important to distinguish between harmonious relations and harmonious perspectives on the world. It is perfectly possible to want, and to achieve, harmonious relations with another person without wanting, or achieving, harmonious perspectives on the world; people can coordinate their lives very well by allowing each other enough of their own "space" (psychological as well as physical space). Assuming that the other person is someone one loves, however, and assuming that loving someone involves some rich and sustained imagining of their point of view, any significant clash of perspectives is going to produce a certain sort of double consciousness.

√ vague

## POSSIBLE SEPARATIONS

Many people will insist that we can regularly imagine the perspectives of those with whom we empathize, without experiencing the inner conflict that characterizes a double consciousness. Our imagining of another person's perceptions and beliefs and desires and feelings, it will be said, can be effectively separated from our own perceptions and beliefs and desires and feelings. We need to look more closely at the nature of the proposed separations in order to evaluate this claim.

Empathy, we have said, requires us to imagine another person's experience from a first-person point of view; we imagine what it is like to experience things the way they do. So even though we are not ourselves afraid of a neighborhood dog, we empathize with a companion who is afraid by creating in ourselves some analog of the companion's experience. There are two distinct ways in which we could try to create an analog of our companion's experience:

1 We could focus on the present scene and try to see the dog *as* dangerous and frightening – by noting its heavy jaw, perhaps, or by finding strangeness in its eyes, or by sensing its weight and its speed.

2 We could imagine a different scene in which the approaching dog really *is* dangerous – a scenario in which the neighborhood dog is foaming at the mouth, perhaps, or a scenario in which it is not the neighbor's dog but a wild dog that is approaching.

Both of these strategies could serve to create a first-person analog of our companion's experience – an experience that involves perceptions, thoughts, and emotions with respect to an approaching dog. Depending on the circumstances (How well can we see the dog? How ambiguous is its behavior?) and depending on the individual (What other dog experiences have we had? How good is our memory?), one or the other strategy may be more successful at achieving empathy. But the nature of the conflict generated by the two strategies differs. In the first case, there is a conflict between experiencing the approaching dog as friendly and experiencing it as dangerous; the scene before us is schematized in two different ways and it is hard to view it both ways at once. We may, of course, continue to *believe* that the dog is friendly, but it now *looks* and *feels* dangerous to us and that is incompatible with it looking and feeling friendly. In the second case, there is a conflict between the look and feel of the perceived situation and the look and feel of the imagined situation; it may be hard to attend and respond to the scene before us while also attending and responding to the imagined scene, but this is a conflict in the allocation of one's mental resources, not a conflict in one's experience of the present situation. The dog before us continues to look and feel friendly even as we imagine a different scenario in which the approaching dog looks and feels dangerous. Since double consciousness requires the application of two different schemas to the same situation, pursuing empathy in the second way will not meet the conditions for double consciousness. As long as we empathize with another person's experience by imagining what it is like to confront a situation that is different from our own, we will avoid double consciousness.

Things are seldom so simple, however, since type 2 imagining often leads to type 1 imagining. Empathizing with a companion's fear (of an approaching dog, say) by imagining a different scenario (a scenario in which one is attacked by a dog) can affect the way we experience the scene before us (making us more attentive to the dog's teeth and the dog's weight, making the present dog look a bit more dangerous that it looked previously). Imagining is like memory in this regard: vivid imagining of non-present situations, like vivid remembering of non-present situations, usually affects the way we perceive our present situation, making it seem more like the non-present situation. (This is just one instance of the effectiveness of "priming".) Again, we may continue to believe that the dog in front of us is entirely friendly, but the dog now looks a bit shifty and just a little wild; and the contrast between our beliefs and our perceptual impressions creates an inner conflict (a conflict between the inclination to welcome the dog and the inclination to stay clear of the dog, for example).

Consider, next, a more significant and extended example of empathy − a case in which your brother's view of social scenes regularly conflicts with your own. Where you see a group of happy and excited teenagers, he sees a group of nervous and inconsiderate young people; where you hear eager voices, he hears strident voices; where you see affectionate nudging, he sees rude pushing. Broadly speaking, this is still a case of conflicting perceptions, for neither party arrives at its different judgments through any conscious inference; to you, the group's happiness is self-evident while to your brother the group's nervousness is self-evident, to you the sound of their voices is eager while to him it is strident. These contrasting perceptions draw on a wide array of judgments and values concerning people's psychologies, cultural norms, and group dynamics and it isn't really possible to imagine your brother's view of the situation from a first-person point of view without also imaging the associated judgments from a first-person point of view. You do not need to endorse these judgments, but you do need to imagine what it is like to judge the situation as he does. why?

Again, there are two ways in which you could do the requisite imagining. You could try to view the scenes you confront as he does (try to see nervousness and rudeness in a group's interactions) or you could imagine somewhat different situations (in which people really are nervous and rude) and suppose that your brother experiences these scenes as you experience those. Only the first possibility has one applying an alternate schema to the same situation, which is a requirement of double consciousness. But, again, imagining of type 2 usually bleeds into imagining of type 1, and insofar as it is not only immediate perceptions but an array of standing judgments and values that must be imagined, the conflict that arises from trying to empathize with your brother while retaining your own independent view will be more significant and sustained.

Not all empathizing has a perceptual component. I may empathize with a student who believes that getting ahead in the world is the most important thing to do – imagining what it is like to make competitive advantage a priority – without imagining different perceptual experiences. But the contrast between type 1 and type 2 empathizing remains: I could imagine what it is like to approach the world in the way that the student does – using money to measure worth, fearing failure, expecting lies; or I could imagine what it would be like to live in a world where money and worth did coincide, where failure was severely punished, and where dishonesty prevailed. As before, only the first sort of imagining meets the requirements for double consciousness, where conflicting schemas are applied to the same situation, but even when we start with imagining of type 2 (where we imagine what it would be like to experience a different world) we usually end up with type 1 imagining (where we imagine experiencing this world differently).

Quite apart from the fact that we usually end up with some amount of type 1 imagining (and the inner conflict that comes with it) even if we start out with type 2 imagining, type 1 imagining is often what we *want* from empathy. If we are afraid of an approaching dog, we want the empathizer to imagine an alternate perspective on the scene before us rather than an alternate world. Their assurance that "I can imagine your experience here because I can imagine what it feels like to be approached by a dangerous dog" is not nearly as satisfying as

"I can imagine this dog looking dangerous". We do not need the empathizer to give our experience the same weight as their own, we allow that they may be tracking information of which we are unaware, and we realize that our outlook may be distorted by past mishaps and mistaken beliefs; but still we want them to see how it is that we could experience this very situation the way that we do. Likewise, if we experience a social group as nervous and rude, we would like an empathetic companion to get herself into a state where the group before us seems nervous and rude to her as well – even though she rejects that take on the situation. And if we equate success with competitive advantage, we would like an empathizer to regard this very world – not some alternate world – in the same way.

Why does it matter? By hypothesis, either method enables the empathizer to imagine what it is like to have our experiences. Why not go with whatever method works best for a given empathizer in a given situation? If it is easier for you to imagine the approach of a different, more dangerous dog than to imagine this tail-wagging dog as dangerous, why isn't that the better way to empathize with your frightened companion? If I can do a better job at imagining a student's frame of mind by imagining myself in a different sort of world, why isn't that the better way to empathize? The answer, I think, is that what we want from an empathizer is not just a reasonably accurate imagining of our subjective state but also, and perhaps more importantly, their realization of how our view could be a compelling alternative to their own. If you can see this very dog as dangerous, you can recognize your companion's as perceptual rather than delusional. However blinkered or biased those perceptions may be, they are still recognized as possible schematizations of information received from the present situation and that gives them an epistemic legitimacy that imagining an alternate scenario does not. The fact that an empathizer is able to experience this very situation in the way we do shows that our experience is grounded in reality (even if our judgments turn out to be mistaken).

Consider an analogous situation in which two people are contemplating a painting. One person sees it as depicting a praying mantis. Even if that person knows they are wrong, they want the other person to try to see it the way they do. Given a choice between having the first person only partially and imperfectly see it as some kind of insect and having the first person quite accurately conjure up the image of a similarly positioned praying mantis, they will choose the imperfect perception over the more accurate imagining. In life, as in art, we want an empathizer to see how things appear to us, and we want them to see how that appearance can be a compelling view of the situation before us. We want them to see how (not merely that) it is possible to see things in a way that conflicts with their own.

There are, of course, cases where we want an empathizer to imagine what it is like to experience a situation that is very different from their own – where the landscapes and the people and the challenges that we face are not the same as those that confront the other person, where we really do live in different worlds (or, more exactly, different parts of the world). In these cases, imagining an alternate situation is appropriate. But, usually, empathy for the experiences of someone in a different situation spills over into empathy for their perspective on a shared situation; and, indeed, that is part of its purpose. So a certain amount of type 1 imagining becomes appropriate after all. Likewise, there are cases of people escaping into a fantasy world – a world which is populated by imaginary characters and scenes, imaginary challenges and dangers – where an empathizer should imagine an alternative world rather than imagine the fantasized characters and scenes as present in the real world. But, again, one of the purposes of such empathy is the insight it provides into the way the other's fantasy life spills over into their outlook on real people and real scenes and real dangers.

Another way to separate our own view from the view with which we empathize, and thereby avoid an inner conflict, would be to entertain just one of these views at a time. When we empathize with someone else, we could put our own view out of mind, and when we pursue our own life, we could put aside the views of others. To some extent, this is exactly what most of us do; we try to give our full attention to others when empathy seems important, and we stop imagining their views when they are gone. With the most important people in our life, however, we find ourselves in a more or less constant state of empathy; we regularly imagine their view of the situations we find ourselves in even as we continue to act on our own. And this is what we want from those who empathize with us; we don't want their empathizing to require a full-attention all-out effort and we don't want them to forget us when we are absent.

If we are right, then, in preferring type 1 empathy and we are right to want our empathy for some others to be significant and sustained, then we are bound to experience some significant and sustained conflicts between our own perspectives and the perspectives of others. By taking the mind of another within ourselves, we ourselves come to be of two minds.

## POSSIBLE DISSOLUTIONS

The third way to eliminate inner conflict was through the dissolution of one or the other position. In the case of empathy, this would mean ceasing to empathize (where empathy requires first-person imagining of someone else's point of view). This wouldn't require us to stop caring for that other person. It would require us to abandon (often unsuccessful) attempts at imagining what it is like to be another person, concentrating instead on supporting their well-being. It would require us to sympathize without empathizing. It would require us to keep the other person "outside" of oneself, avoiding the inner conflicts that result from taking them "within".

There are reasons to think that keeping other people "outside" of ourselves, sympathizing but not empathizing, will result in better knowledge of other people and better treatment of other people. Reviewing these arguments will help distinguish between cases where empathy (and its attendant conflicts) is worthwhile and cases where empathy is better avoided.

What, exactly, is the difference between gaining knowledge of another person's state of mind through empathy versus gaining knowledge of another person's state of mind through observation? Empathy, as we have stated, requires first-person imagining of another person's state of mind.[10] If we already know that someone is afraid of dogs, or that someone views life as an endless competition, we can try to imagine what it is like to have those fears, or to have those views; and this can give us first-person knowledge where previously our knowledge was third-person. First-person imagining of another person's emotions or beliefs in a given situation can lead to further first-person imagining of their actions in that situation, of their emotions and beliefs in another situation, of their likely response to a future event, and so on. On the assumption that this further imagining is governed by the same rules or forces (rational or physiological) that govern the other person's emotions and beliefs and actions, it can give the empathizer further knowledge of the other person's mental states. In contrast, when we rely on observation, we maintain a third-person perspective and collect evidence about another person's situation and behavior and we arrive at a hypothesis about the person's current state of mind – based on whatever theory best accounts for the collected observations.[11] For many years, there was an animated dispute about which of these methods is normally used. The first story about how I come to understand you has been called the Simulation Theory while the second story about how I come to understand you has been called the Theory Theory. Eventually, important concessions were made on both sides of the debate. Defenders of Simulation Theory acknowledged the role of observation and theory (largely unconscious) in guiding one's imagining – i.e. in effecting the transition from information about another person's situation and behavior to an associated state of mind. Defenders of the Theory Theory, on the other hand, acknowledged that most of the relevant theorizing occurs automatically as soon as we begin to imagine (what it is like to be in) another person's circumstances. As a result, the focus of interest within cognitive psychology shifted to different models of the unconscious processing that results in the prediction and attribution of mental states to others.[12]

If we focus our attention on cases where we are consciously trying to gain knowledge of another person's mental states – where unconscious processing does not take me, immediately and confidently, to a conclusion about what you are thinking and feeling – then the difference (and the conflict) between knowledge through empathy and knowledge through observation reasserts itself. Different schools of acting, for example, advocate conflicting methods – some asking would-be actors to vividly imagine themselves in the situation of the character they are portraying, others teaching would-be actors to observe, analyze, and carefully replicate the behavior of people like the character they are portraying. Likewise, different schools of anthropology advocate different methods for studying the norms and practices of other cultures – some recommending maximal immersion and identification with those studied, others adhering to a scientific method that insists on the collection of quantitative data uncontaminated by expectation and interpretation. And, in our very ordinary lives, as we pass a beggar or listen to a friend, we are often pulled between the stance of empathizer and the stance of analytic observer.

On behalf of empathy, Philip Koch complains that "without it we would experience others only as objects, lacking any sense of what has to be called their 'presence'" (Koch 279). But the analytic observer, no less than the empathizer, is trying to understand the mental states of other people – not just the likely movements of an inanimate object; whether an absence of fellow feeling helps or hinders in understanding the mindset of others is precisely what is at issue. Following the lead of many different languages, we could distinguish two different senses of understanding – one empathic, the other more observational.[13] But insofar as both are trying to arrive at a correct view of another's point of view – a correct characterization of their perceptions, their beliefs, their desires, their feelings, their expectations – they are different methods for gaining knowledge of other minds, and it is appropriate to consider their relative success in achieving that goal.

It is reasonable to suppose that empathy produces more accurate attributions when the person one is trying to understand is a lot like oneself – not only with respect to personality and dispositions but also with respect to life circumstances and memories (background information). The more different the other is from oneself, the less reliable the outcomes of empathy. The justification for this supposition is simple: what anyone would think or feel or do in a given situation depends on their background beliefs, their standing dispositions, and their values; so if my beliefs, dispositions, and values are much like yours, I will be more likely to think, feel, and do the same as you – and otherwise not. It is easy for me to empathize with my sister facing financial difficulties, much harder for me to empathize with a teenager living on the street. This suggests that empathy is the best method for understanding people like ourselves while cool observation and theorizing is the best method for understanding people unlike ourselves. This simple conclusion is complicated by the difficulty of determining relevant versus irrelevant similarity, by the ever-present possibility that we are wrong about ourselves and thus wrong about others like ourselves, and by the probability of empathizing itself being guided by theory. If we believe that people are all more similar than not, that we usually understand ourselves pretty well, and that empathy is guided by theories that have passed the test of time, then we might favor the empathetic method in all cases. On the other hand, if we believe that people are always unique, that we are often self-deceived, and that our unconscious or instinctive theories are often wrong, then we might want to avoid the empathic method in all cases. (It is also the case that some people are better than others at imagining, and thus at empathetic understanding.) More relevant to our concerns, though, is the implication that empathy is appropriate in just those cases where there is not any significant conflict between the other person's view and our own, and that when there is such a conflict it is better to rely on third-person observation and theorizing. If this is right, though, it means that the only others that we ought to try to "take within" are those whose outlook does not conflict with our own in any significant way.

Empathy is valuable for things other than acquiring knowledge of the contents of another person's mind, however. Often, we already know what someone else thinks or feels or intends to do (they've told us, or we have made some good inferences on the basis of our observations), but we want (and they want us to) know *what it is like* to have those thoughts and feelings and intentions; we want (and they want us to) share their experience. And even when our differences mean that our first-person imagining of another person's mental states is deficient, taking them "on" in this way can serve to stretch our own imaginative capacities and challenge our own convictions – effects that are familiar to anyone who has been in a long-term relationship.

Empathy is also thought to be morally beneficial insofar as it motivates us to act on another's behalf. But does it? Critics of empathy as an aid to morality have raised the following objections:

(1) Empathy makes too many mistakes about others' states of mind, and thus about what is in fact beneficial to them.

(2) Empathy favors those who are most similar to ourselves, which is contrary to a morality that extends to all.

(3) Empathizing with those who are suffering actually makes us less likely to act on their behalf because we instinctively want to avoid situations that we find distressing.

There is merit in each of these objections, but none of them should make us abandon empathy altogether. Objection 1 should encourage us to rely more heavily on third-person observations and theorizing to gain knowledge of another's mental states (especially when there are significant differences between ourselves and that other); but it shouldn't stop us from empathizing on the basis of what we do know. Objection 2 should alert us to the danger of restricting the scope of morality to those with whom we can empathize; but it doesn't mean that empathy can't be a powerful tool in the service of morality.[14] Objection 3 should alert us to those cases where we turn our back on another's need because of the discomfort caused by our imagining of their suffering; but it shouldn't blind us to the many other cases in which the discomfort caused by our imagining of another's suffering is an important part of what moves us to action.

## THREE MODELS, AGAIN

In previous chapters, we described three models for living with the inner conflict of double consciousness: the model of juggling, the model of isometrics, and the model of the disrupter. What do each of these models suggest for the particular form of double consciousness addressed in this chapter – namely, the double consciousness that results from our sustained imagining of another person's contrasting perspective?

When only one of the perspectives that combine to form a state of double consciousness is one's own (the other belonging to someone else with whom we empathize, either automatically or deliberately), what would it mean to juggle between the two perspectives? Unlike the Mexican-American who embraces a dual identity, the empathizer endorses only one of the views she lives with. I may have internalized my mother's religious outlook, but I think it is mistaken; you may empathize with your fearful companion, but you think her fear is inappropriate; we may empathize with another generation's view of the world, but we reject it. Although sustained empathizing can create an inner conflict that is worth retaining, shouldn't one party to that inner conflict (the Other within) remain in the background, never actually displacing one's own perspective (thus unlike the way that one ball temporarily displaces another when juggling)?

This sounds right, but there is an important difference between displacing endorsement of one view with endorsement (however temporary) of another and displacing a commitment to act on one view with a commitment to act on another. When we juggle dual identities (Mexican-American, philosopher artist, etc.), we move back and forth between conflicting endorsements and conflicting commitments to action; in the case of empathy, on the other hand, we may juggle between acting from our own point of view and acting from the point of view of the other – without ever endorsing the other's point of view. Out of respect for my mother, for example, I might participate in a prayer or a hymn – without for a moment endorsing the premises of that prayer or hymn. (I am not thinking of a case in which I merely pretend but, rather, a case in which I enter into the "spirit" of the activity out of empathy and respect.)[15] Similarly, out of care for your frightened companion, you may move away from an approaching dog – without ever yourself doubting that the dog is harmless. One could make such accommodations without empathizing with the other's views, of course, but if there is ongoing empathy then the relevant accommodations will typically involve some inner juggling between adherence to one's own view and imagining the view of another.

A second model for living with double consciousness was the model of isometrics – a model in which the conflict between opposing forces is intensified as a way of strengthening each of the opposing positions. Here the application to cases of sustained empathy is pretty straightforward. Keeping an alternate to one's own view of things in mind can help to clarify one's own view, for often we don't know just what we think or feel or intend until we try to distinguish it from what someone else thinks or feels or intends with regard to the same situation. It is not until your brother describes a group of teenagers as nervous and rude that you realize that you view them instead as excited and affectionate. The outlook of one generation comes into sharper focus when it is contrasted with another. Clarifying the distinction between one's own view and someone else's can also be a way of becoming more secure in one's own view ("Now I know what I think"), and leaning into the distinction ("I do *not* share the views of my parents!") can strengthen one's commitments. (Constant awareness of opposing views can also weaken our commitments and dissolve the opposition. But, having already argued for the desirability of the double consciousness that comes with empathy, I am describing one model for its retention.)

As in physical isometrics, intensifying the opposition between one's own position and that of another can also, somewhat ironically, create a stronger bond between the two. This is true for several reasons. First, as before, each side may depend on the other to define itself, to provide the contrast that is necessary for discerning the contours of one's own view. Second, the energy that goes into opposing another view is also an indication that one cares about that view and considers it important. Being cared about and considered important is often what matters to us most in a relationship, so even antagonistic expressions of that care can strengthen the bond between people. Third, conflict tests relationships and severe conflict tests relationships severely; but discovering that a relationship can survive the conflict gives assurance of its long-term stability. (In the case of an internalized Other, ending the relationship is not usually an option. But noting its survival in the face of conflict can still be reassuring.) None of this means that we should intensify the conflicts in all relations with others; but for those cases where internalization or empathy is either inevitable or worth preserving, the isometrics model does suggest a way to approach and to appreciate the resulting conflicts.

The third model for living with double consciousness was the model of the relentless disrupter. Disruption, it will be recalled, can be embraced as an antidote to complacency, as resistance to the dominance of any one view, or simply as a way to keep things interesting. Applied to the kind of double consciousness described in this chapter, the disrupter model would have us welcome conflict with an inner other as a way to jog us out of our own established point of view. Continuing to imagine the point of view of a different person would serve as a way to dislodge our fundamental categories and assumptions so as to make our lives more fluid and less oppressive.

There is a problem, though, with adopting this model in the case where our double consciousness stems from a conflict created by imagining another person's point of view. Much as their view may be a more or less constant presence for us, it is not accepted as our view. In the case of double consciousness resulting from a dual identity (like that of a Mexican-American, or a philosopher artist), where both points of view are embraced as one's own, the continual disruption of one identity by another identity may be an appealing way to keep one identity from dominating over another. But when the second identity is that of another person, with views that one explicitly rejects, taking it on as a way of disrupting one's own

*Trump's* [handwritten annotation]

view would mean displacing one's own identity with that of someone else. Apart from worries about the rather arbitrary nature of the changes this would involve (whatever alternate viewpoint we happen to internalize or empathize now becoming our own), this suggests a rather bizarre sequence in which the very distinction between self and other disappears. For, first, one would adopt the other's point of view in order to undermine the stability and complacency of one's own; but then, having made that view one's own, one would switch to yet another view (perhaps revert to one's previous view, which now functions as the new other) and so on. Meanwhile, if the other with whom we empathize is proceeding in the same way with respect to ourselves, they will displace their initial point of view with ours just as we replace ours with theirs. While there are good reasons to question overly sharp distinctions between self and other, this strategy would make nonsense of the distinction between self and other, and it would transform our attempts to empathize with others into opportunities to take on new roles.

Of the three models we have been exploring, then, the juggling model applies with some restrictions on just what is being juggled, the isometrics model seems promising, but the disrupter model cannot apply without destroying the self–other distinction that is fundamental to the double consciousness described in this chapter.

# **Four**

> It's the vastness, and the smallness, that makes this possible. So intense are my feelings; yet the circumference seems to make a hoop round them. No, I can't get the odd incongruity of feeling intensely and at the same time knowing that there's no importance in that feeling.
>
> (Woolf 344)

Virginia Woolf wrote these lines as she reflected on her writing about the Bloomsbury art critic Roger Fry, in 1940, when a German invasion of Britain was imminent. The inner conflict she experiences is a familiar one – the conflict between finding a current passion intensely gripping and regarding it as totally unimportant in the larger scheme of things. The very same situation – her writing about Fry – is schematized in two different ways, one focused narrowly on the challenges and pleasures of her writing project, the other focused broadly on the irrelevance of such biographies in a time of war. When Woolf writes that she "can't get the odd incongruity of feeling intensely and at the same time knowing that there's no importance in that feeling", she is not expressing a puzzle about what the difference is, or about how one might move from one of these views to the other. Rather, she is expressing her inability to bring the two views into some sort of harmony. This sort of clash does not depend on the particulars of Woolf's writing project nor does it depend on the imminence of a war, for no matter what one is engaged in doing, there is always some wider perspective from which it will look unimportant. When we hold onto both a narrower and a wider perspective on our various endeavors, we will frequently find ourselves of two minds about the importance of what we are doing.

## THE BASIC CONFLICT AND ITS INESCAPABILITY

Thomas Nagel has long maintained that there is a fundamental divide between a subjective standpoint and an objective standpoint, and that we ought to hold onto both without trying to unify them into a single point of view.[1] Nagel thinks that we confront this divide when we try to understand an alien form of life (his example is a bat) through extensive study of their physiology, their behavior, their conditioning, and their evolution, without ever coming to know what their experience is like "from the inside". But Nagel is also interested in the subjective/objective divide as it affects one's thinking about what is important and what is worth doing, and it is this aspect of the topic that will concern us in this chapter. In *The Possibility of Altruism*, for example, Nagel addresses the need to accommodate the special way that we value our own life alongside the moral demand that we recognize the equally valuable lives of others.[2] And in his essay "The Absurd", Nagel juxtaposes the local importance of our endeavors with their cosmic irrelevance. To abandon the wider, impersonal perspective would leave us governed by our most immediate and selfish concerns – living a life like that of simpler animals. But to abandon the narrower, personal perspective would dissociate us from our embodied existence – living a life like that of a transcendent god. Humans, according to Nagel, must have access to both perspectives, but these perspectives can never be integrated into a single coherent point of view. Instead, he suggests, we must learn to live with a foot in both camps, retaining both a narrower and a wider view of ourselves and our situation.[3]

It is worth noting that the wider view that most of us hold alongside the narrower is a view which makes our narrower concerns seem *less* meaningful rather than meaning*less*. When we stand back and view our situation within the larger picture, our influence on others is very small but it isn't nothing; when we adopt a wider point of view we see that local politics or saving one tree makes very little difference, but we don't see that it makes no difference at all. This is not just a fact about the wider perspectives we actually take; it is a fact about what is required in order to take up any perspective at all. There can't be any point of view at all without meanings – i.e. without ways of categorizing things, and ways of evaluating things with respect to those categories.[4] So while it makes perfect sense to view our local concerns as relatively unimportant from a wider point of view, it makes no sense to suppose that we can occupy a point of view from which our lives have *no* meaning.

Nagel is especially convincing in his rejection of compromise solutions to the tension between narrower and wider points of view.[5] There will always be a narrower view from which our pursuits seem important and a wider view from which they seem unimportant, and settling for something in between would deprive us of both sides of what makes us human – our devotion to our individual pursuits and our recognition of their relative unimportance in the larger scheme of things. Quite apart from the difficulty of locating the appropriate midpoint (Should Woolf view her writing from the point of view of literary history? From the point of view of English security? From the point of view of human civilization? From the point of view of our solar system?), maintaining a middle-distance perspective promises to weaken one's enthusiasm for one's endeavors while also restricting the scope of one's reflections. This does not mean that we ought to adopt the narrowest possible view alongside the widest possible view, but only that enjoying both narrower and wider perspectives on our lives is an important part of being human.

What about a subsumption of one perspective by the other? Why can't one's smaller, local concerns be subsumed within larger, global concerns, even as narrow slices of a scene get subsumed within the wide?[6] The goods in my life are only a small part of what is valuable in the universe, but they are part of it nonetheless. Minor events, furthermore, can have major effects – greater than anyone can predict, so the potential value of any one act should not be discounted.

The problem with this strategy for overcoming the tension between narrow and wide views of what is important is that it simply discounts the narrower point of view in favor of the wider, or it rejects the legitimacy of any value comparisons whatsoever. Putting aside the question of whether anything at all seems important when we consider the universe as a whole (I return to this question later), viewing one's narrower concerns as a tiny part of what is important in the world as a whole is bound to make those narrower concerns look a lot less important – effectively eliminating rather than incorporating the urgency and the passion one feels from the narrower point of view. That is the first horn of the dilemma. Alternatively, if one retains the sense that very local concerns are important by insisting that they actually could have a major impact on the world at large, then one must plead ignorance about the relative value of everything – effectively undermining all value comparisons. That is the second horn of the dilemma.

Consider the case of an individual's suffering. How important is it, really? As Dorothee Sölle points out:

> Certainly the suffering of the proletarian masses is objectively more important than that of a single artist. But this kind of "objectivity," applied consistently, destroys the capacity to perceive any suffering at all. Every unity can be relativized and minimized over against a greater whole. In the total span of world history sufferings evaporate as it is. It is a macabre spectacle to draw up a balance sheet that ranks people's sufferings in order of importance.
>
> (Sölle 106)

Sölle is not denying the legitimacy of the wider view of human suffering, but she is rejecting the attempt to subsume the narrow view under the wider view through the use of a quantitative scale that measures their relative importance. If we subsume the "subjective" importance of an individual's suffering under the "objective" importance of the world's suffering, the importance of an individual's suffering (or an era's suffering) is minimized to the point where we can no longer perceive it as important at all, and when we can no longer perceive the importance of an individual's suffering we can no longer perceive the importance of any suffering at all.

The same dilemma arises when we compare short-term outlooks versus long-term outlooks with regard to a single life. Often, these aims pull us in opposite directions. We can "be in the present" or we can take the long view. Spending the day studying might serve one's long-term interests while watching an entertaining movie serves one's short-term interests.

Staying silent in the face of an offense might bring long-term satisfaction while lashing out provides short-term satisfaction. Examples of such conflicts are numerous, and it is tempting to suppose that short-term satisfactions can be subsumed under the long-term satisfactions of a life well-lived. But viewing spontaneous and short-term pleasures as just one part of a longer good life diminishes our ability to give ourselves over to the moment, experiencing it as the only thing that matters. (Watching a movie becomes a sensible break rather than a moment outside of time, and a temper tantrum becomes a useful release rather than a dive into the abyss.) Or, alternatively, if one supposes that every experience makes some unknown contribution to the larger good (or bad) of life, then the assumed contrast between short-term goods and long-term goods becomes unintelligible.

The contrast between long- and short-term interests is echoed in the contrast between reflective and unreflective stances. For long-term satisfaction typically depends on long-term planning, and long-term planning requires one to adopt a reflective stance towards one's life. Short-term satisfaction, on the other hand, typically depends on pursuing one's immediate inclinations without becoming reflective about them. Bringing unreflective states under the umbrella of reflection tends to destroy, not preserve, their unreflective character and the satisfactions that come with it.

If the conflict between narrow and wide perspectives (or short- and long-term perspectives) can't be resolved in any of the ways canvassed earlier, there is still the possibility of ending the inner conflict by separating the domains or the contexts for which we adopt a narrower perspective from the domains or contexts for which we adopt a wider perspective. While being human may require us to occupy both narrow and wide points of view, certainly there are situations in which we should restrict ourselves to a narrower or a wider perspective. For activities that require a great deal of focused attention, for example, maintaining a wider as well as a narrower perspective can be counterproductive. If you are performing a difficult surgery, or maneuvering a dangerously heavy piece of furniture, or counting the number of geese in a flock (it is not the importance of the activity but the concentration it requires that is relevant), then doubling one's state of mind with the addition of a wider perspective is not usually wise.[7] Similarly, for activities that depend on having very quick responses – stopping someone from being run over by a car, or catching a falling glass, or watching for the moment a frog flicks its tongue, it is better to restrict oneself to a narrower view.

There are also activities for which a narrower perspective should be abandoned in favor of a wider point of view. These tend to be mental as opposed to physical activities, since physical activities require us to be attentive to our local position (what it is that we are trying to do, where we are in space and time).[8] They also tend to be activities that, by their very nature, are addressed to larger and longer-term concerns – making policy decisions that call for impartiality, for example, or thinking through the implications of a black hole in a distant galaxy.[9] It would be a mistake, however, to suppose that a wider perspective is the more important perspective, or that a wider perspective is always more relevant when it comes to matters of importance. Mental activities are not always more important than physical activities, and longer-term consequences are not always more important than short-term consequences – not within a life, not within politics, and not within science.

There are many areas of our lives where it is either impossible or undesirable to restrict ourselves to a narrow point of view or a wide point of view. Pursuing a career or raising children, for example, require a nearly continuous balancing of narrower and wider perspectives, with narrower concerns often appearing quite unimportant from a wider point of view, and vice versa. And while it might be wise to forego the wider perspective while filling out a form or driving a child to school, most of the activities that go into a career or that go into raising a child both demand and benefit from the ongoing presence of both perspectives. Taking each individual endeavor too seriously – treating it as all-important – threatens to undermine the effectiveness of one's actions just as much as does refusing to take anything seriously – treating it all as unimportant. But what, exactly, does it mean to sustain this particular form of double consciousness?

### THE OPTION OF IRONY

Irony is Nagel's favored response to the tension created by holding onto both a narrower and a wider outlook. There are many different types of irony, but they all depend on presenting a point of view while dissociating oneself from that view; it signals a critical distance from the claims that one makes, a disowning of the thing that one puts forward.[10] Irony is fashionable – not just in academic circles but in youth culture and in contemporary media. The popular band U2, for example, has been admired for the way that it uses the brands, slogans, and images of pop-culture in a way that mocks them – managing to be a part of pop-culture while simultaneously criticizing it.[11] Ironic parents – indulging their children while rolling their eyes at themselves, and ironic careerists – doggedly pursuing their goals while continuously mocking their own aspirations, are familiar figures in the social landscape. On the face of it, irony is a way of juggling narrower and wider perspectives, keeping both in play without denying the conflict. Whereas the act of juggling depends on keeping each "ball" alive, however, the stance of irony tends to deaden both points of view – draining the narrow perspective of its energy and absolving the wider perspective of the responsibility to act in any way. This can be seen in both the theory and the practice of irony.

A noted theorist of irony with respect to the conflict between narrower and wider perspectives is Richard Rorty. Rorty describes the internal conflict that arises when one combines adherence to one's own schema (what he also refers to as one's own "vocabulary") with the realization that from a wider point of view that schema is no more compelling than its alternatives (other "vocabularies"). Because meaning and justification are always relative to a particular schema, it is impossible to compare the relative worth of competing schemas from any further, neutral point of view (or "vocabulary").[12] Even the articulation of conflict must be done from within the standpoint of one schema or another. But there are plenty of cases in which encounters between alternate schemas lead to serious political clashes and there is no wider perspective from which such clashes can be mediated. Rorty's recommended response to this situation is a stance of irony – a stance in which we continue to adhere to our own schema while recognizing that it is no more justified than that of our opponent. In the context of war, this might mean fighting for our own side while acknowledging that our opponent is equally justified. In the context of rhetoric, Rorty advocates a private rhetoric that condemns alternative points of view alongside a more public rhetoric that promotes tolerance and inclusion. Needless to say, this strategy creates an uncomfortable tension (if not outright hypocrisy) between public and private rhetoric, and Rorty has come under heavy criticism for some of its implications.[13]

The worry I want to raise is a bit different. Rorty's irony weakens our commitment to both the narrower and the wider view – our commitment to the vocabulary we use for ourselves and other like-minded people, and our commitment to the vocabulary we use to communicate with others. On the one hand, regarding our own cause as no more justified than any other cause is bound to undermine our motivation to pursue that cause; and on the other hand, regarding our more inclusive talk as a public front rather than a personal conviction absolves us of any responsibility to make it more than just talk. Rorty recognizes the danger of teaching irony to our children, who would then lack all conviction, but he fails to explain how adults are supposed to circumvent the same dangers. (He also suggests treating "nonintellectuals" as children: "In the ideal liberal society, the intellectuals would still be ironists, although the nonintellectuals would not" (Rorty, "Private Irony and Liberal Hope" 87). Perhaps enabling them to fight the wars that intellectuals only talk about?) Applied to the situation that Woolf finds herself in, a Rorty-like approach might have Woolf privately (but doubtfully) enthusing about her own witty writing while publicly (but emptily) speaking in favor of the general good of mankind.

I find Rorty's sort of irony unappealingly smug and complacent. It represents a kind of know-it-all stance that is foreign to Woolf's struggle; it possesses a kind of I-can-have-it-both-ways confidence that Woolf lacks. Such complacency could result from a lack of emotional engagement with the larger picture (it is hard to imagine Rorty as disturbed by the cultural wars as Woolf is disturbed by World War II); or it could signal overconfidence in the power of conceptual distinctions (Rorty is a philosopher, after all). Instead of being genuinely ambivalent – that is, actively pulled in opposite directions – his type of irony is contentedly two-faced. And in that sense, it is a deadening rather than an enlivening form of double-mindedness.[14]

## JUGGLING AND DISRUPTING, LESSONS FROM LAUGHTER AND SURREALISM

In seeking an alternative to irony, it is instructive to compare some different ways in which laughter negotiates the tension between narrower and wider perspectives. For laughter often depends on our ability to juxtapose inside and outside perspectives on an issue or event. Our narrower obsession with the color of a shoe, for example, or the cost of a sandwich, becomes laughable when viewed from a broader perspective. Humor often relies on our ability to see ordinary concerns and ordinary disputes from the point of view of someone with a wider view of the matter.[15] (Helmuth Plessner (1970) makes the interesting suggestion that the physical shaking that comes with laughter is a manifestation of our oscillation between inside and outside points of view, expressing the tension between our attempts to remain in control of our lives and our acceptance of a loss of control.) But there are different styles of laughter – different ways of playing the wider off the narrower. The laughter analog to Nagel's ironic stance, I suggest, is a wry, resigned sort of laughter – a look-down-from-on-high, smilingly indulgent shake of the head. The laughter analog to Rorty's ironic stance is a more conspiratorial laughter – a we-can-get-away-with-something kind of mirth. As I've already indicated, I find both of these stances too smug and too complacent. The laughter analog to Woolf's style, on the other hand, is more disorienting – more like the continual back and forth of juggling. (This sort of laughing is also closer to crying – a similarity that Plessner pursues in some detail.)

Consider the extreme of hysterical laughter. Often such laughter can be understood as an involuntary expression of the mismatch between one's immediate, more subjective view of things and a wider, more objective view of things. Indeed, one definition of madness is the inability to coordinate one's subjective view of one's situation with a more objective view of that situation.[16] Louis A. Sass describes schizoid patients as prone to both "intense subjectivism and hyperobjectivism" (37), manifested, for example, in the distinctive laughter of patients contemplating their own experiences from the point of view of their minders.[17] But we don't need to be mad to experience a mismatch between our own view of what we are up to and another's view of what we are up to as "hysterically" funny – as when an attempt to improve something can be seen, within the wider context, as only making things worse. When the subjective/objective gap becomes too extreme, or too uncomfortable, however, there is a tendency to discount the legitimacy of one or the other of these perspectives (even as one keeps both in mind), or to oscillate uneasily between the two perspectives. Sass describes

> the sardonic and off-putting yet somehow perplexed irony of patients who feel profoundly alienated from any normal activity or human encounter – who may, for example shake hands as it they were engaging in some totally absurd and arbitrary action or may respond to questions as if condescending to petty and useless demands.
>
> (112)

Or, alternatively,

> a vacillation among perspectives, a shifting among worlds, each with its own form of articulation and separateness, and where the confusion, when it occurs, stems from a kind of vertigo, a continual collapsing of one frame of reference into the next.
>
> (136)

George Eliot, in *Middlemarch*, remarks on a similar juggling of narrow and wide perspectives: "Strange, that some of us, with quick alternate vision, see beyond our infatuations, and even while we rave on the heights, behold the wide plain where our persistent self pauses and awaits us".[18] Her bemused observation includes a temporal contrast, between short- and long-term interests ("infatuations" versus a "persistent self") and a spatial contrast ("the heights" versus "the wide plain") to distinguish the emotional ruggedness of landscapes viewed close up from the broader calm that comes into view when our vision is broadened. Her imagery is the reverse of more standard representations, however, in which the wider, more encompassing perspective is located "above" a narrower, more restricted perspective. In this passage, Eliot places the wider perspective "below" – presenting it as the common ground from which more fleeting and idiosyncratic passions will sometimes rise up.[19]

The fact that we can imagine wider perspectives as residing either higher or lower than narrower perspectives does not mean that the association of wider perspectives with higher perspectives is completely arbitrary. There is a long tradition of associating high class, high culture, high courts, and high mindedness in general with perspectives that are broader and more impartial – i.e. more objective. And there is an equally long tradition of treating the wider perspective as the more valuable perspective. In opposition to these traditions, there are notable attempts to reverse the hierarchy, placing greater value on the lower class, low culture, and lowly pursuits – because we ought to put a higher value on what is more local and earthy and particular, or simply because this side of the opposition has been shortchanged.[20] (Adam Gopnik maintains that "the quality of irony that we value today is . . . the habit of turning objects and values upside down, of seeing big and little inverted" (Gopnik 29).) Here the aim is not so much a perpetual juggling of opposing perspectives but, rather, a determined disruption and displacement of whatever perspective is dominant at a given time by whatever perspective is oppressed or occluded by the dominant one.[21]

Recent advocates of deconstruction, following Derrida and others, have been influential promoters of this tactic in politics and in the arts. But their commitment to disruptions and inversions can be found in the earlier, and equally influential, school of surrealism. The term "surrealism" indicates adherence to something that exists below ("sur") what is standardly regarded as the real; but it also marks an inversion of what counts as real. What was previously deemed unreal and unimportant (the world of dreams and fantasy) is now viewed as most real and most important, and what was previously viewed as the broader, more objective part of our experience is now viewed as a very narrow part of what matters to human beings in general. The original surrealists were well aware that the contents of our subconscious are bound to change as our social and political conditions change. André Breton, for example, visiting Haiti in 1945, linked the aims of surrealist art and the aims of the impending revolution, insisting that both psychological and political freedom "must be thought of not only as an ideal but also as a constant re-creation of energy. It must exclude all ideas of comfortable balance and instead be conceived as continuous rebellion" (Breton 1). Twenty years later, Octavio Paz wrote:

> I have no idea what the future of the surrealist group will be. I am certain, however, that the current that has flowed from German Romanticism and Blake to Surrealism will not disappear. It will live a life apart; it will be the *other* voice.
>
> (Paz 55)

What makes surrealist disruptions particularly relevant to the topic of double consciousness is their reliance on uncomfortable juxtapositions as a way to dislodge dominant assumptions and ideologies. The surrealists insisted on the liberation of suppressed realities (both psychological and political) but resisted any attempt to create new forms of order. (Their political sympathies were more anarchist than communist, for example, and they were critical of institutionalized psychiatry.) In his manifesto of 1924, Breton advocated "a juxtaposition of two more or less distant realities. The more the relationship between the two juxtaposed realities is distant and true, the stronger the image will be – the greater its emotional power and poetic reality". Not just any juxtaposition will suit the aims of surrealism, however. The juxtaposition must be between a familiar reality and a reality that upends that familiarity. Surrealist painting presents ordinary objects with extraordinary characteristics – refusing any unified identity (humans with bird beaks, watches that melt, an elephant made of machine parts). Surrealist humor (which can be found in absurdist literature and theater and music as well as the visual arts) works by introducing some normal expectations and then pursuing bizarre and irrational deviations from those expectations. But whereas the normal and dominant assumptions were initially taken to be representative of a wider, more objective reality, it is the abnormal and countervailing assumptions that dominate the surrealist's reality.

### THE ISOMETRICS ALTERNATIVE

Isometrics was our third model for managing double consciousness (the other two being juggling and disruption) – a model whereby increasing the tension between competing perspectives actually strengthens both. As we saw before, Woolf "knew" that within the wider world situation there is no importance to her feelings about her writing. But she then goes on to ask: "Or is there, as I sometimes think, more importance than ever?" Could it be that a wider view of things reveals the narrower view to be more rather than less important? And, vice versa, could it be that a narrower view adds to rather than detracts from the importance of a wider view?

With respect to Woolf's situation, it is possible to imagine how invoking the wider view of a world at war could make the narrower view of her writing project seem more rather than less important – much as a grove of trees seems more important in the midst of a dessert or a small island seems more significant when surrounded by a vast sea. Woolf's writing may have offered her a psychological antidote to a larger despair, and it may have seemed like the one thing she could do to counteract (in however small a way) the destruction of the world that she valued. There are plenty of everyday examples of this response. Recognizing how little control we have over the life of a child or a friend, we might decide to be even more dedicated to the little that we *can* do. Faced with political dysfunction on a massive scale, one might get more involved in local politics. Discouraged by global threats to the natural world, one might become more attentive to and protective of the natural world at hand.

Nagel seems to dismiss this response as self-indulgent. Reflecting on Camus's admiration for a defiant Sisyphus, who continues to roll a rock up a hill despite its ultimate futility, he writes: "This seems to me romantic and slightly self-pitying. Our absurdity warrants neither that much distress nor that much defiance" (22). But this sounds like skepticism regarding enthusiasm of any sort, a shrug of "whatever" from someone who is already bored. Why shouldn't the despondency generated by a wider view intensify rather than deplete our commitment to a narrow view? Perhaps because Nagel views the narrow and the wide view as equally true or valid, he will object to any response that favors one over the other. (He rejects the option of suicide, for example, as a kind of concession to the wider view.) But the isometric model suggests that we can use the conflict to intensify and deepen both positions. We have seen how holding onto a wider view might actually strengthen our commitment to a narrower view, but could holding onto a narrower view also strengthen our commitment to a wider view? Could focusing on the importance of our particular projects and passions also add to our appreciation of their greater unimportance?

The pleasures and pains of our narrow pursuits can be both intense and erratic, and the more invested we are in these pursuits the more intense and erratic the emotions that come with them. The suffering and instability that this creates can create a kind of backlash that adds to our investment in a wider view – a view from which our particular travails matter little, and the ups and downs of our lives even out over time. Just as a wider sense of meaninglessness can lead to a defiant reaffirmation of a narrower view, a narrower sense of emotional chaos can lead to a determined reaffirmation of a wider and calmer point of view. On at least one version of the Buddhist ideal of non-attachment, we humans ought to pursue our particular tasks and interests, suffering the emotional turmoil that inevitably comes with them, while also occupying a wider perspective that detaches us from that turmoil. While the state of "non-attachment" might sound like a state in which we carry on in a rote, affectless way, various passages in the *Bhagavad Gita* insist not only on the inevitability of emotions such as anger or grief but also on their appropriateness. A common understanding of non-attachment according to the *Gita* distinguishes between emotions as disturbances that pass through us and emotions as orientations that control us or define us, recommending that we accept the former but reject the latter. Put another way, we are asked to remove the ego from the emotion. What does this mean? One suggestion is that we should allow ourselves to be moved by our emotions, but we should not allow ourselves to linger on those emotions; another suggestion is that we should carry out our particular duties with great commitment, but we should not care whether we succeed or not.[22] Either way, the stresses of a narrower view drive us toward a wider view while the wider view supports our ability to persevere with the narrower view. (Non-attachment is supposed to make Arjuna stronger in his warrior role.)

I find this version of mutual strengthening of narrow and wide viewpoints plausible but not appealing. I don't doubt that people can counter the emotional disarray of narrower pursuits by adopting a stance of non-attachment while also relying on that stance to strengthen one's commitment to the narrower pursuits. But the recommended stance of non-attachment seems extremely abstract and unengaging, while the engagements in narrower pursuits seem complacent and unimaginative. Reflecting on the current popularity of Buddhism in Western societies, Zizek (First as Tragedy) notes how it

> enables you to fully participate in the frantic capitalism game while sustaining the perception that you are not really in it, that you are well aware how worthless the whole spectacle is, since what really matters is the peace of the inner Self to which you know you can always withdraw.
>
> (66)

I think there is another, more attractive version of isometric strengthening between narrow and wide points of view. In this version, the wider view is a view that ranges across much more of the spatial and temporal landscape, but it is a view that does not abstract from the details of that landscape so much as it fills them in, and it is as emotionally engaging as the narrower view.[23] Instead of a grand gesture towards the cosmos as a whole, we can dig into the details of cosmic history, of subatomic particles, of other solar systems, of black holes. Instead of using a wash of pale colors, Veronese-like, or a disappearing blackness, ala Caravaggio, to create the background for a chosen scene, we can fill in that background in meticulous detail – so much so that, Bruegel-like, no one scene takes on any special importance, yet the whole comes vividly alive by virtue of the provided detail. Instead of broadly alluding to a country's history of poverty and violence, we can give a detailed history of its people's movements, rituals, diseases, wars, and economics.[24] In the case of Virginia Woolf, writing in 1940, the wide view could include a very detailed understanding of the impending war (its causes, its costs, its victims, its rulers), making the background of her writing a site of intense emotional engagement.

It is not hard to see how attending to one's narrower pursuits could lead from one detail to another onto a greater interest in the details of a wider view. Looking for the causes of a particular event leads one ever-further back into history; looking for the reason for a particular opinion leads one ever-deeper into the assumptions of an entire culture; looking at the pattern of a particular leaf leads one to be curious about lots of other plants; and so on. Attending to the details of a longer span of history, a broader culture, or a wider range of plants can also motivate a closer, narrower look at particular events, assumptions, and objects. The two views, narrower and wider, may compete for our attention at any given time but keeping them both in mind strengthens our involvement in each. I cannot study one particular worker in a Bruegel painting while also attending to the painting as a whole, but keeping the wider view in mind as I attend to the narrower (and vice versa) adds to my knowledge and appreciation of each. The wider view is not a view from which the narrower seems unimportant, but its importance looks different in the context of a wider array of details. The tiredness of one worker is juxtaposed with the rest of another, the load on one person's back with the bobbing in water of another – making the whole into a tapestry of ordinary life in which the intensity of each moment is set off by the intensity of various other moments, and we experience the whole as something more complete and more alive than any one detail on its own.

Something similar, I suggest, might happen if Woolf could see her involvement with her own writing as just one of many equally intense pieces of a larger tapestry. From the wider view in which thousands of people are dying and many more are struggling, Woolf's writing project is relatively unimportant, of course; but it is precisely the intense feelings and life pursuits of individual people that makes the impending war so important, so Woolf's feelings and pursuits are vividly illustrative of what matters and what is at risk in the wider view. When she wonders whether, perhaps, her feelings have more importance than ever, she could be wondering whether it is the intensity of human feelings – regardless of what feelings they may be, and regardless of whose feelings they may be – that makes the war so significant.

Does this overcome conflict at the level of feeling? Not necessarily, but now the conflict is no longer a conflict between feeling that things do matter and feeling that they don't matter, between caring and not caring (where those two feelings could be mutually reinforcing only insofar as they each continue to defy each other). It is, rather, a conflict between the feelings that come with caring about something as an individual thing and the feelings that come with caring about it as a part of something larger. To the extent that a pursuit is valued because of its contribution to something larger (as when one's job is valued because of its contribution to a war that one believes in, or when one's care for a child is valued on account of its contribution to human history), the feelings elicited by the narrower view will not conflict with the feelings elicited by the wider view. But there are numerous cases where an object or an event matters to us independent of any larger cause to which it contributes, or where what matters to us in the short term conflicts with what matters to us in the long term. We dislike doing certain tasks even as we take pleasure in the way they advance a larger project, we delight in the pleasure we give to our children even as we worry that we may be spoiling them, we are sad about a parting but happy about the larger implications of that parting, and so on.

Many emotions are bound up with judgments that are not justified, or that are justified from one point of view but not another. Anger involves the judgment that one has been wronged, but that judgment may not be justified by one's evidence, and what counts as having been wronged may look different from different points of view. For Richard Rorty, the wide point of view is a point of view from which questions of justification can't arise (since justification only makes sense from within one or another narrower point of view); the double consciousness of his ironic stance therefore consists in a narrow perspective from which certain actions and certain emotions are justified plus a wider perspective from which justification doesn't make any sense. It is no surprise, then, that Rorty's wider perspective is purely intellectual, lacking an emotional counterpart. The wider point of view I have been recommending, however, is a point of view from which a given action must get its justification from considerations that extend across a much wider swath of space and time – much wider than the range of considerations immediately at hand. This doesn't eliminate justification, and the emotions that depend on justification, but it does create situations in which what is justified by narrower considerations is different than what is justified by wider considerations, and the emotions that are appropriate from a narrower point of view are inappropriate from a wider point of view. From a narrow point of view it may be appropriate to be angry with a robber, while from a wider point of view it may be appropriate to be compassionate (or vice versa); from a narrow point of view being amused by a prank may be justified, while from a wider point of view disgust may be appropriate (or vice versa).

Again, an isometrics model suggests that opposed feelings are often strengthened by the opposition. The bitter can be more bitter when juxtaposed with the sweet (and vice versa), the joy can be more intense when conjoined with grief (and vice versa), the amusement can be greater when there is also disgust (and vice versa). Once we have rejected the imperative to harmonize all of our feelings and to overcome states of double consciousness, it becomes possible to use the opposing forces of our psychology to strengthen rather than weaken each other.

## CLOSING REMARKS

The combination of narrow and wide perspectives is one of the most common types of double consciousness that we live with. Occupying both perspectives is an inescapable part of being human insofar as we must be engaged with our immediate surroundings but also be aware of a larger world beyond those surroundings. I have argued against various attempts to overcome or avoid the conflict between these two perspectives – by subsuming one under the other, for example, or by adhering to just one at a time. I have also argued against some standard ways of living with the conflict. Irony, in particular, has become a popular way of dealing with the tension between narrow and wide perspectives, with different forms of irony recommended by different philosophers. Thomas Nagel and Richard Rorty advocate two different forms of irony which I find rather dispiriting. So I have explored some alternatives – first through a consideration of different forms of laughter, and second through a consideration of wide perspectives that are more emotionally engaging than those described by Nagel and Rorty. As in previous chapters, the models of juggling, disruption, and isometrics point to some promising ways to embrace rather than resist this everyday form of double consciousness.

# Five

Study as if you were going to live forever; live as if you were going to die tomorrow.

This simply-stated instruction, attributed to Maria Mitchell,[1] is actually quite difficult to understand and even more difficult to follow. Since we are not going to live forever nor (in all probability) are we going to die tomorrow, Mitchell is recommending that we base our outlook on falsehoods – one falsehood when studying, another (contradictory) falsehood when not studying. It seems safe to assume that she is not urging us to *believe* either of these falsehoods, however, not even temporarily; the falsehoods are supposed to *guide* the way we live without actually deluding us.

## THE ROLE OF FANTASY IN EVERYDAY LIFE

In order to appreciate the subtlety of Mitchell's advice, it is useful to consider an overly simple reading of what she is saying: whenever we are studying, we ought to ignore the fact that we will eventually die and, at all other times, we ought to ignore the fact that we will probably live for many more years. In both situations, a fairly ordinary fact about the likely span of one's life is supposed to be kept out of consciousness.

The problem with this reading is that it fails to capture the *as if* character of the recommended states of mind – the sense in which Mitchell is recommending a kind of *pretense* rather than a kind of willed ignorance. Just what kind of pretense this is, and why it is important to the way we live (and not just to the way we play) is the subject of this chapter.

There is a difference between avoiding knowledge of a particular fact by refusing to "look" (or by "looking" the other way) and pretending that a contrary fact obtains by imagining that it is true. Avoidance creates a blind spot while pretense cultivates an illusion. I can ignore the fact that my child is mad at me by restricting my attention to other aspects of my environment; or I can pretend that my child is not mad at me by imagining her being calm and affectionate (rather than irritable and withdrawn) and I can act in accordance with that imagined scenario. Both strategies can be beneficial – enabling parent and child to move past a problem – but they rely on different mental acts. Normally, in the case of avoidance, a certain amount of mental effort must be expended in order to keep a belief out of consciousness. In cases of pretense, on the other hand, mental effort must be devoted to imagining a possibility that is contrary to what one believes to be true.[2]

I read Mitchell's recommendation to study as if one were going to live forever as a recommendation that, when we are studying, we imagine that we are immortal – not just turning a blind eye towards our eventual death but, more actively, imagining an infinitely extended future for ourselves. This imagining may be more or less substantive, with more or less details filled in by the imagination, but in order to have an influence on the way one thinks and acts the imagining cannot be entirely "empty". It is not enough merely to introduce the idea of immortality; one must imagine the implementation of that idea in experience, conjuring up at least some of the experiences that would accompany its actualization.[3] To imagine that I will live forever, I would have to conjure up experiences such as the following with some degree of accuracy: having time to pursue hundreds of different options rather than just a few, always having the option of changing my mind and starting all over, being able to observe the future effects of a present event, never needing to rush in order to finish a task, and so on.

Mitchell is not recommending that we engage in a fantasy of immortality *alongside* the activity of studying (something that would amount to a distracting daydream) but, rather, that we use the fantasy of immortality to help *guide* the activity of studying, to better orient us as we study. The perspective of immortality is supposed to be brought to bear on the activity of studying – even while we continue to believe that we are in fact mortal. Drawing on a fantasy of immortality, a student might become less anxious about her slow pace of learning or about the extent of what she doesn't yet understand. When studying math, the fantasy of immortality could create a sense of timelessness that gives one more patience for following out more implications of a given theorem. Or when studying politics, the fantasy of immortality could prompt one to attend to longer term effects of an event or policy – changes that will take effect a hundred years from now.

Likewise, to follow Mitchell's advice to live as if one were going to die tomorrow, one must actively imagine that one will die tomorrow and one must bring that imagining to bear on one's current concerns. It is not enough to say "Yeah, I suppose I could die tomorrow"; one must go on to imagine some of the implications of that scenario – the end of various endeavors, the impact on one's family, the elimination of certain worries, and so on. The imagined scenario, moreover, must be brought to bear on one's current activities, the prospect of an imminent death altering one's perspective on one's present life – highlighting the relative unimportance of some pursuits, the inappropriateness of some reactions, the urgency of some tasks, and so on. The intended effect of Mitchell's advice is, presumably, to live our lives with greater appreciation and a better sense of proportion.

To live as if things were other than one knows them to be has some similarities with the state of a child pretending that a stick is a pony, or that her doll is sick. The pretending child sustains a double perspective on some object or situation – imagining that the stick is a pony while recognizing that it is not a pony. Like the student studying math as if she were immortal or living as if she were going to die tomorrow, the child's fantasies about her situation alter her interactions with her surroundings, with some of those interactions governed by the fantasy and others governed by what she believes to be true. The fantasy of dying tomorrow does not lead one to send out notices to one's friends, and the fantasy of riding a pony does not cause worry when the stick fails to bend its legs. There is seldom a clear line between the actions prescribed by the fantasy and the actions prescribed by one's beliefs; however, should the student's fantasy of immortality lead her to ignore bodily needs (while studying)? Should the child offer water to her stick? Indeed, such interactive forms of pretense will often generate an inner conflict – between treating the stick as a pony and treating it as a stick, or between caring for a doll as if it were sick and dismissing it as mere plastic. This is not a conflict between belief sets, as it was in cases discussed in Chapter 1, for example, since the fantasizer is perfectly aware that her fantasies are mere fantasies; rather, it is conflict between the different perspectives that one uses to guide one's actions.

Isn't there a difference, though, between indulging our fantasies during playtime and relying on fantasies when engaged in real-life pursuits like studying or meeting friends or going for a walk? While it is fine to offer water to a stick while playing, why should we want fantasy to have a say in how we go about learning and making life decisions? While it is fine to treat a stick as a donkey in a game of make-believe, why treat it as anything other than a stick when it comes to real life?

Before addressing these questions head on, let me introduce a few more examples of the kind of double consciousness I am calling "as if" living.

*Hospital as forest:* Jack lies awake in a hospital, unable to sleep on account of his pain, worry, and various noises on the ward. In order to counter his agitation, he begins to listen to the noises as if they were sounds in a forest – as if they were the sounds of falling leaves, singing birds, creaking trunks, wind in the pines, and so on. He studies the IV poles as if they were saplings covered in vines. He attends to the nurses as if they were unusual animals. He responds to his own pain as if it were caused by the physical challenges of the forest – the stab of a broken branch, the sting of nettle, the ache of endless walking, and so on. He does not attempt to escape into a fantasy that is disconnected from his actual surroundings so much as he attempts to respond to his surroundings as if they were something else.

*Swimming as praying:* Ollie is an atheist who often goes swimming in a cold ocean. Whenever she enters the water, she imagines herself entering the nave of a stone monastery and she reaches out her arms as if she were bowing in prayer. She focuses on her breathing as if each breath were a message sent to god. She feels the water flowing around her as if it were the holy spirit encompassing her in its energy. When she exits the water, she touches the water in a closing gesture of thanks, and if she begins to shiver, she treats it as if it were the sign of a successful exorcism.[4]

*Car as animal*: Sid calls his car Stripe and talks to it as if it were an animal, perhaps even human. "Where shall we go today, Stripe?" "Was it hard to wait in the sun?" "Don't worry; I'll be back soon". If Stripe gets scratched, Sid imagines that his car is an animal that feels pain, and he pats its side as if to offer comfort. But he doesn't look to see if it is bleeding, say, nor does he wonder whether a local anesthetic would be helpful. When Sid is around other people, he keeps his remarks to himself or he makes his voice sound much sillier than it sounds when he is alone with Stripe.

Each of these cases is rather commonplace, and not particularly puzzling. Such fantasizers are perfectly aware of the falsity of their imaginings; they are not deluded. Neither are they trying to delude themselves into believing falsities – to replace their present beliefs with beliefs that they consider to be false.[5] So what are they up to?

Like the play of children, these fantasies can be fun and they can offer a welcome escape from the demands of ordinary life. But these fantasies have an additional purpose: they serve to generate appropriate responses to one's real-life situation. In each of the prior cases, as in the cases addressed by Mitchell, a fantasy is invoked in order to improve these people's responses to their actual situation. In the case of Jack, the desired response is greater calm and fewer value judgments. In the case of Ollie, the desired response is a steadier focus and a greater dedication to her chosen activity. In the case of Sid,

**Why It's OK** to Be of Two Minds

the desired response is a greater sense of connectedness and ease with his car. Unlike the case of pure play, where actual objects (sticks, dolls) are used as props or stand-ins for various fantasy objects (a horse, a person), in the case of "as if" living, it is the fantasy objects (trees, a church, an animal) that serve as props or stand-ins for actual objects (poles for intravenous drips, a lake, a car). One is not using reality to further one's interactions with a fantasy but, rather, one is using a fantasy to further one's interactions with reality.

The improvements in one's interactions can be more than practical – not just conducive to one's happiness or one's effectiveness in doing whatever one is doing. "As if" fantasies can also further our knowledge if the imposition of a false image or story on a true state of affairs reveals truths that would not otherwise be recognized. To see how this might happen, consider the case of metaphorical language and metaphorical thought.

Metaphor is the non-literal application of a concept. The concept of a swamp is applied to national politics (which is not something that literally can be a swamp); the concept of a hawk is applied to a presidential candidate (who, literally, cannot be a hawk); the concept of a fire is applied to a desire (which, literally, cannot be a fire); and so on. Many such applications are intended to draw attention to properties that a thing actually has – the hard-to-escape corruption of Washington, a legislator's quickness to support lethal interventions, the overwhelming intensity of a feeling. Although there are many competing theories of just how a metaphor works, it is generally agreed that metaphors can provide us with fresh insights through their suggestive reorganizing of attention. By attaching an image to some aspect of a person or situation ("her mind is a sponge", "the meeting was a minefield"), a metaphor can make those aspects more memorable. But also, and more importantly, good metaphors can disclose aspects of a situation that would not otherwise be recognized. Referring to a group of adolescents as "tea cups" can cause others to see their fragility and their sense of their own importance; describing a daffodil as "whipped butter" may draw attention to the previously unnoticed texture of its petals; and so on. We rely on falsehoods to reveal truths.

Similarly, in cases of "as if" living, a fantasy may serve to redirect our attention to an overlooked (or underappreciated) aspect of our situation – the variety of pitches within the noise of a hospital ward, for example, or the quiet that exists underwater. Still, acquiring new insights is not the central aim of the fantasies cited earlier; those instances of "as if" living do not reveal new truths about our world so much as they enable us to occupy conflicting perspectives on our surroundings – one serving the interests of truth, the other serving the interests of fantasy. Whereas saying that the stars "stream" across the sky draws our attention to the true fact of their continuous movement alongside each other and in a single direction, saying that they "shake with laughter" invites us into a particular fantasy about their outlook on the world.[6]

Throughout this book, I have been defending *persistent* forms of double consciousness. The preceding examples of "as if" living seem to be fleeting rather than persistent, however. We expect Jack and Ollie and Sid to revert to a single truth-based point of view after their brief cultivation of each fantasy. It is not difficult, however, to imagine each of them continuing with their double consciousness for much more extended periods of time. Jack realizes that his forest fantasy can help to counter his irritable response to background noises even after he leaves the hospital, so he gets in the habit of reconfiguring all sounds in light of that fantasy. Ollie decides that "spiritualizing" her experiences enriches her life and makes her a nicer person to be around, so she extends the images of traversing a monastery far beyond the time she spends swimming. Sid enjoys talking not only to his car but to pretty much everything he interacts with – his clothes, his food, his toothbrush, his pillow. The reasons in favor of their short-term indulgences in fantasy carry over to long-term indulgences in the same fantasies.

One might worry that persisting in these fantasies across too many cases for too long will transform "as if" living into delusionary living. This is a fair worry, but it needs some unpacking. On the one hand, if one is able to sustain a perspective based in perception alongside a perspective based in fantasy, and if one recognizes the fantasy to be a fantasy, then it shouldn't count as a delusion. On the other hand, insofar as one's fantasy serves to guide one's thoughts and feelings (and, indeed, is valuable for precisely that reason), then we might wonder whether the fantasy has become a kind of belief – which, because false, amounts to a kind of delusion. Multiple criteria may be invoked when deciding whether (or not) a person actually holds a particular belief – verbal expressions (or denials) of that belief, actions that conform (or fail to conform) with that belief, feelings that are explicable (or not) by that belief.[7] I am not interested in debating boundaries for what should be called a "belief"; I am interested in cases where it is beneficial to be guided by what one knows to be a fantasy (e.g. that I will live forever, that I am in a monastery, that my car is an animal).[8]

## COMPARISONS WITH PHYSICS AND MATHEMATICS

Physicists sometimes emphasize the inevitable falsity of their current theories – either because those theories contain clear contradictions, or because those theories, like all theories before them, are sure to be replaced by very different theories in the future. Yet their calculations, and their actions, and indeed their imaginations are guided by their current theories; their theories may be false, but they are useful – useful for interacting with the world and, perhaps, useful for arriving at truer theories in the future. Some prefer to say that the physicists' theories are instrumentally true, but unless one simply equates true with useful (in which case one should simply call them true)[9] it is more accurate to refer to them as useful falsehoods. The examples of "as if" living discussed earlier are also useful falsehoods but, unlike the case of the physicist, we use them despite our knowledge of what is in fact true (e.g. that I will die, that I am in the water, that my car is not alive).[10]

Likewise, when people choose to believe something comforting or pleasing because (they think) there is no way of knowing what is actually true, they are not in a state of double consciousness. Consider the following remarks on New Age healing practices:

> I know that a polished red rock is not going to heal my tailbone. It's not going to bring my mom back either. It may not do a thing. But none of us know anything about anything, really. So why not be open to the possibility of hope?

> (Burton)

This writer chooses to believe in the power of crystals because (she says) there is no way of knowing what is actually true. (Her assertion that there is no way of knowing what is actually true actually conflicts with her claim that she knows that the rock is not going to heal her tailbone or bring back her mom; but a sympathetic reader could interpret this to mean that she is aware of the claims of science yet, given its uncertainty, she chooses to base her beliefs on the "religion" of astrology.) If we take her at her word, this writer is not of two minds; rather, she has replaced a belief that she used to consider true with a belief that she considers most useful for her pain, and for her mood.

Mathematics provides a closer analogy to the double consciousness of "as if" living that we have been discussing. The relationship between different series of numbers can be usefully represented spatially, with a graph or a geometrical figure, despite the fact that numbers are not themselves spatial. Consider how a line representing the series 1, 2, 3, 4, etc. rises slowly and steadily while a line representing their squares 1, 4, 9, 16, etc. curves upward more and more steeply; or how a rectangle can usefully represent the result of 8 multiplied by 14. We often rely on graphs and figures to guide our thinking about investment potentials, say, even as we recognize that quantities of money are not quantities of space. Reliance on such representations in math is analogous to our examples of "as if" living insofar as, in both cases, we choose to be guided by an image that is misleading even when (unlike in the case of physics) we have other, less misleading representations at our disposal – i.e. we can rely on algebra rather than geometry when dealing with non-spatial things.[11]

There are some important differences, however, between our reliance on spatial representations of non-spatial relations when we are doing math and our reliance on religious representations of non-religious relations when we are swimming, or our reliance on animal representations of inanimate things when we are driving. First, in the case of mathematics, the translation of non-spatial facts into spatial images is quite precise and rule-governed. A doubling of what is non-spatial must correspond to a doubling of what is spatial, an increase or decrease in number must be reflected by an increase or decrease in size, and so on.[12] For this reason, we can rely on geometrical images to improve our ability to reach algebraic conclusions; they enable us to see more relations more quickly, which (usually) improves the speed of our calculations and our ability to spot inconsistencies.[13] When we imagine swimming as a visit to a monastery, on the other hand, or when we imagine a car as our pet, there is a lot more leeway as to what does or does not get represented (the waves? the horizon? the steering wheel? the color?) and there is a lot more freedom with regard to how things get determined (should the horizon be the city outside the monastery or a wall of the monastery? should the car's steering wheel be the animal's brain stem or its leash?). This difference means that, unlike the case of geometrical representations of algebraic relations, we cannot expect to use images of an animal to make discoveries about the workings of a car.

Second, and more importantly for our purposes, the use of images in "as if" living differs from the use of images in mathematics insofar as "as if" living uses its distorting imagery *as* a distortion; the projected fantasy is *meant* to be misleading, to pull us away from rather than towards a truer view of our situation. Although (like metaphors) the imagery of "as if" living can be used to highlight certain truths, that is not their primary function. And although (like daydreaming) the fantasies of "as if" living can have considerable entertainment value, that is not its primary value. "As if" *living* is a way of *acting* in the world; the relevant imagining affects not only our thoughts and feelings, but also our actions. So the value of the imagining that supports "as if" living will include the value of acting as if the world were different than it actually is.

We have already described how acting as if we will live forever might mean that we study more patiently, how acting as if we are in a monastery might mean slowing our pace and staying focused, and how acting as if a car is a pet might mean being more protective towards it. Each of these effects could, of course, be pursued more directly – without the intervention of a misleading fantasy; but relying on a fantasy can be a more efficient and more effective way to change one's behavior. Holding onto a compelling image is often easier than continually reminding oneself to behave in a certain way (retaining the image of a monastery is easier than repeatedly telling oneself to slow down and stay focused), and it is often more effective as well (the image of an animal is a better motivator for protectiveness than the directive "take care of your car"). Acting as if the world were different than it actually is, then, can lead to behavior that is better suited to the way the world actually is.

In the remainder of this chapter, I want to consider some cases of "as if" living that are more pervasive and more important than those discussed so far – cases that have generated significant philosophical controversy and confusion: the case of performing an identity, the case of treating people as if they had free will, the case of viewing values as if they were objective, and the case of regarding people as if they were unified. These are complicated strategies that emerge from complicated contexts, and what I have to say will be limited. Still, I hope to show how the distinctions and reflections from the first part of this chapter help clarify the nature and value (or disvalue) of each of these kinds of "as if" living.

## PERFORMING AN IDENTITY

It has become common to think of various aspects of one's identity – one's gender, for example – as something that one performs rather than something that one has in any intrinsic, let alone essential, way.[14] The idea that gender is a type of performance became popular through the work of Judith Butler, following the publication of her book *Gender Trouble: Feminism and the Subversion of Identity*, where she argues that people acquire their gender identities through the repetition of behaviors that define their place in social space. Butler then introduces parody (evident in drag performances, for example) as a way to subvert the power of those identities, to loosen the grip of those behaviors, and to upend the restrictions of the social space. By becoming aware of performances as performances, we can occupy two competing perspectives simultaneously – one in which we partake in a particular identity and one in which we disown it. We can act as if we were female while refusing to be female.

One simplistic response to this position is the following: Our identities are not separable from our actions; what we do establishes who we are. Across time, therefore, there can be no distinction between performing a particular identity and having that identity. This response is simplistic insofar as it obliterates the possibility of an ongoing distinction between inner and outer life (while ongoing participation in disingenuous acts does tend to alter one's character in the direction of those acts, sometimes a mask is just a mask); and it is simplistic insofar as it overlooks the distinction between reflective and unreflective points of view (what one does automatically may not square with what one believes upon reflection). Viewing one's own gender as a performance could be like the outlook of a waitress who takes on the role of waitress constantly aware that her performance is merely a mask, knowingly adopted for the sake of her job. Or it could be like being a "team player" who is only intermittently reflective enough to recognize that he doesn't actually identify with the relevant team. In the first case, one doesn't experience a clash of competing perspectives, one simply engages in disingenuous acts. In the second case, one mostly avoids the sense of conflict by foregoing reflection on one's behavior.

I take Butler to be advocating a rather different stance, however – a state of genuine double consciousness in which (unlike the pretending waitress) we really do hold competing perspectives on our situation and (unlike the unreflective team player) we continue to be aware of the conflict.[15] It is a state in which the gender that one performs is simultaneously owned and disowned – a state in which (unlike the pretending waitress) one fully inhabits a particular gender identity while also (unlike the unreflective team player) one continues to regard it as a fantasy. Butler's exemplar of this double stance is the drag queen who simultaneously affirms a female identity and advertises its artificiality, who becomes female through a caricature of femininity. (Much more could be said about what it means to own versus disown a particular identity. My own view is that self-ownership depends on the integration of beliefs, feeling, and actions; so simultaneously owning and disowning a particular identity depends on both pursuing and resisting certain efforts at integration.)

Much as I respect Butler's insights about gender and the states of double consciousness that gender identities can provoke (not just the performance consciousness discussed previously, but also experiences of being both male and female), I want to distinguish constructed identities from what I have been calling "as if" living. Constructed identities may rely on fantasies for inspiration, but (as the term "constructed" suggests) they transform those fantasies into realities. The construction may rely on a fantasy to disguise the fact that it is a construction (the fantasy of an essential, pre-existing identity), but that doesn't make the constructed identity any less real.[16] "As if" identities, on the other hand, use fantasies to guide one's thoughts and behaviors without transforming (or even supposing that one is transforming) those fantasies into realities. Imagining that I am male may help me turn into a male, but imagining that I am a bird won't help me become one. I can construct a male identity, but I can only live "as if" I were a bird.

Performing an identity, then, can mean either of two things. It can mean embracing a particular way of conceptualizing various aspects of oneself in full knowledge that that conceptualization does not reflect one's underlying nature so much as it reflects a socially useful way of organizing and directing people's attention. Alternatively, "performing" an identity can mean acting as if one were something that one knows one is not. The advantages and disadvantages of constructed identities tend to be more social and less manageable. Conceptualizing certain militants as terrorists empowers some and disempowers others, and it is seldom under the control of any one individual. Partly because it exists in opposition to social expectations and norms, living as if one were immortal is a more individual option, and more under one's control.

### TREATING PEOPLE AS IF THEY HAD FREE WILL

Most people regard most adults as having at least some degree of free will and therefore having at least some responsibility for being kind rather than cruel, for obeying rather than disobeying the law, for sticking with a job rather than abandoning it, and so on. Yet many insist that we are the products of chance and circumstance, so free will is merely a useful illusion.[17] So they continue to treat people as if they had free will while denying that that free will actually exists. This is a significant example of "as if" living. Why preserve the illusion, and what are the alternatives?

One argument in support of the illusion of free will starts with the claim that we cannot hold people responsible for what they do unless we suppose that they have free will. If a person's state of mind is dictated by their biology and their circumstances, then they are not responsible for what they think and feel and do. Either biology and circumstances are responsible, or there is no such thing as responsibility – things just are as they are. Yet holding people responsible for what they think and do is socially useful: it encourages us to punish and therefore deter wrongdoings, it teaches children to monitor themselves, and it prevents us from feeling helpless in the face of evil, for example. So, the argument goes, we are wise to preserve the illusion of free will even though it is merely an illusion. And as long as we continue to recognize that it is an illusion, this means that we are wise to remain in a state of double consciousness with regard to the existence of free will.

One alternative to living as if we had free will would be to punish wrongdoing, teach self-monitoring, and counter helplessness simply because these are useful things for a society to do. Being responsible might be reduced to being someone that society finds useful to reward or punish (without any appeal to the presence of a free will); or the notion of being responsible might simply be abandoned. The problem with this alternative, for many of us, is the fact that it replaces distinctively moral attitudes with merely practical calculations. Autonomy or self-directedness stops being an end in itself; it becomes, at best, a means to the creation of an ideal society. Praise and blame are no longer justified by the rightness or wrongness of a person's act; they are justified by the practical effects of these reactions on society as a whole. Respect for individuals as individuals is replaced by approval (or disapproval) of the conditions that made them who they are. Instead of regarding each other as moral agents, we regard each other as more-or-less successful contributors to the continuation of humankind.

Suppose then that living as if we had free will is necessary for distinctively moral (versus merely practical) attitudes. What, exactly, is the fantasy of a free will? Most of the fantasies discussed in this chapter have been fairly easy to describe and fairly easy to conjure up in imaginative detail: fantasies of living forever, fantasies of dying tomorrow, fantasies of being in a forest or a monastery, fantasies of living machines. Indeed, it is the specificity of our imagining that enables our thoughts and feelings to be effectively guided by the fantasy, to proceed as if the fantasy were true. In comparison with those examples, the fantasy of a free will is extremely elusive, and necessarily so. Free will is not the kind of object that could be perceived, nor does it have the kind of properties that could be perceived. Free will is defined by the absence of external causes, and even if it is possible to perceive causal relations it is not possible to perceive the absence of causal relations.[18] Insofar as free will can be imagined, it must be imagined in an abstract, purely cognitive way. That sort of imagining, though, cannot provide us with an alternate experience of (versus idea about) our situation; it is not really "thick" enough to guide "as if" living.

Nonetheless, I think it is possible to imagine ourselves as agents (perhaps spirits) that observe the world and act on it without being affected by it. This is no more difficult than imagining a god with the same powers – imagining that can be problematic in any number of ways (how can a god perceive the world without being affected by it? how can a god act on the world without disrupting its causal laws?), but no more problematic than imagining that cars are animals. Indeed, on many accounts, we are like a god precisely insofar as we have a free will. For better or for worse, then, living *as if* we had free will would be living as if we were a god that is free to disrupt the otherwise deterministic nature of the universe. For an atheist this can be a significant kind of "as if" living; it draws on a fantasy to support the sort of moral regard that we want to extend to each other.

## VIEWING VALUES AS IF THEY WERE OBJECTIVE

Skepticism about the objectivity of values is even more common than skepticism about the existence of free will. (It is easier to construe free will in such a way that it is compatible with determinism than it is to construe the objectivity of values in such a way that values depend on human judgments.) There is some interest, however, in the benefits of living as if (at least some) values were objective even while believing that they are not.[19] Again, I am not here interested in the reasons for advocating such a stance (usually having to do with the greater motivational force of values that we believe to be objective). I am interested in what it would mean to live as if certain values were objective and whether this amounts to an important form of "as if" living.

It helps to consider a concrete example. Suppose I believe that generosity is good and greed is bad but I deny that there is anything *objectively* better about a generous person or objectively worse about a greedy person (or, for that matter, anything objectively good about there being any people at all). I believe that these judgments of good and bad are merely reflections – or projections – of my preferences (and, perhaps, those of many other people).[20] But suppose, also, that denying the objectivity of these values always makes me feel depressed about the world, alienated from others, and less inclined to cultivate generosity and resist greed. I might then try to view these values *as* objective even though I believe them to be subjective preferences only. More specifically, I might choose to imagine generous people as having the intrinsic property of goodness (much as I might imagine apples as having an intrinsic property of redness) – despite knowing that there is no such intrinsic property.[21] Likewise, I might imagine greedy people as entirely lacking in that property, or as possessing an equally intrinsic property of badness. By imagining things in this way, I am better able to act forcefully and confidently in my attempts to increase generosity and decrease greed, and I feel better about myself overall.

There are a couple of ways in which this could work that would *not* produce "as if" living. First, I could succeed in deluding myself. I could set myself up to believe something contrary to my initial beliefs – through immersion in appropriate contacts and reading, for example; or I could try to silence my more philosophical reflections whenever dealing with these particular values. But the end result would be a changed consciousness, or a submerged consciousness, not a double consciousness. Second, I could merely pretend that the goodness of generosity and the badness of greed are objective properties. I could talk as though goodness and badness were properties that I could perceive directly (even though, in fact, I could not perceive them) and I could act like I am more confident than I actually am. Unless the pretense infiltrated the way I actually experienced generosity and greed, however, the pretense would be merely an act, a case of public misrepresentation rather than a case of "as if" living.

To constitute a case of double consciousness, we would need to view generosity as good only insofar as we approve of it and, simultaneously, to view generosity as possessing a simple, intrinsic property of goodness. This combination seems considerably more difficult than the case of experiencing a hospital as if it were a forest, or experiencing a swim as if it were a visit to a monastery. In the case of the hospital and the forest, many different aspects of the hospital can be "translated" into aspects of a forest. To regard the fairly elaborate property of society approval as a simple red-like property, on the other hand, requires one to ignore the complexity – to look the other way, as it were, and thereby to create something that is closer to a state of delusion than a state of double consciousness. Furthermore, in the case of the hospital and the forest, the patient's imagination locates the fantasy objects (birds, trees, wind) in the same place as their actual counterparts (voices, chairs, the whir of machines). This convergence of location is important, I think, to the success of the imaginative endeavor. Imagining that there is a simple property of goodness in the generous person, on the other hand, depends on locating that property in a very different place than one believes it to be in fact. While we may be successful in maintaining the fantasy of an objective goodness alongside the belief in its subjectivity, it is hard to see how the fantasy could be superimposed on the real world in such a way as to guide us in our dealings with that world.

## REGARDING PEOPLE AS IF THEY WERE UNIFIED

A final candidate for "as if" living, and one that reflects back on the topic of this book – double consciousness – is living as if people were unified while believing that they are not. In many cases, and for much of the time, people actually are unified. But Chapter 1 argues against the necessity of a unified consciousness, and much of this book is devoted to identifying ways in which a lack of unification is desirable. The option of regarding others as if they were more unified than they are remains open, however. Thomas Nagel sketches an argument against the unity of consciousness (based on findings from patients who have had their corpus callosum severed) but he also emphasizes the importance of the idea of a unified consciousness for our ability to empathize with others. If the consciousness of others is not unified, then neither is mine, and that makes it impossible for "me" (what me?) to imagine myself as "you" (what you?). Insofar as the ability to empathize with others is central to morality, then, the illusion of a unified consciousness may be a very useful illusion.[22]

As Nagel describes it, "the illusion consists in projecting inward to the center of the mind the very subject whose unity we are trying to explain: the individual person with all his complexities" (163–164). Although I question whether empathy depends on such a projection, I agree with Nagel's analysis of the illusion, and I think that living as if people had such a center (while accepting that no such center actually exists) constitutes an important sort of "as if" living. We regularly imagine a self that is a kind of focal point in the center of people's heads (or, in some cultures, the center of their chests), and we are guided by that image even as we believe it to be a false image. One effect of imagining the self (or soul) as such a center is that it bestows a unity on others (and on ourselves) that is at odds with the evident disunity of a person's behavior. This can be advantageous insofar as it provides a simple (if imaginary) target for our respect, for it is hard to extend respect to all of the messy and conflicting aspects of a person. Similarly, imagining the self (or soul) as a unified center in the midst of mental disunity is advantageous in that it invites us to think of people as extremely stable; the center can hold even if its surroundings change. Viewing people in this way can help to alleviate our worries about what someone will do or think or feel, and this may be useful towards building (unearned) confidence in ourselves as well as others.[23]

Living as if people are unified (while believing that they are not) certainly is possible, then, but it is not always advisable. After all, there will be circumstances in which withholding respect is more important than bestowing it, and there will be circumstances in which making accurate predictions is more important than assuming stability. Furthermore, even if psychological unity tends to increase stability, there will be cases (like the ones I have been describing in this book) where consciousness is unified around two distinct centers and is less stable as a result. Indeed, the ability to hold onto two perspectives simultaneously may be a sign of greater rather than lesser stability. Finally, in general, a person's ability to live with a foot in two different cultures (Chapter 1), keep a past perspective in mind even as one lives in the present (Chapter 2), to empathize yet keep one's separate identity (Chapter 3), and to sustain a broader perspective alongside a narrower perspective (Chapter 4), is something that might add to rather than diminish the respect we extend to that person. Thus the usual reasons for living as if people are more unified than they actually are do not carry over to these cases of double consciousness.

This book has described some types of inner conflict that we have good reasons to preserve – indeed, to relish – rather than try to eliminate.

Almost everyone experiences the five types of inner conflict addressed in the five chapters of this book. While the conflicts are more intense or more difficult for some people, they are familiar to everyone.

First, it is common to identify with two or more different cultures – different ethnic cultures, different religious cultures, different job cultures, different generational cultures, and so on – and there are times when our allegiances to these various cultures pull us in different directions. This is the type of inner conflict that is often referred to by the term "double consciousness", but it is just one sort of double consciousness.

A second form of double consciousness occurs as we age. Over time, most of us undergo significant changes in outlook – changes in what we consider interesting or worthwhile, changes in how we understand other people, changes even in what we are able to perceive. Recalling a past outlook in vivid detail can produce another kind of double consciousness in which we experience the world through our past "eyes" as well as through our present "eyes", creating an inner conflict between the self we once were and the self we are now.

Third, when we imagine how things seem from someone else's point of view, and when that person's point of view becomes a regular part of our own inner life – their criticisms running through our minds as we go about our business, their preoccupations distracting us from our own – then conflicts between ourselves and others become inner conflicts as well.

Fourth, as human beings we are capable of standing back from our local concerns to take a wider view – to reflect on the larger significance or, more often, the larger insignificance of our actions. Projects and our passions that feel urgent and important from a narrower point of view appear passing and trivial from a wider point of view. This too puts us at odds with ourselves since we value both narrower and wider points of view.

Fifth, and finally, most of us engage in various fantasies to help guide our lives – fantasies about benevolent spirits, for example, or fantasies about free will – even when we believe them to be mere fantasies. Once again, the result is a common form of double consciousness in which we continue to approach the world through conflicting frames of mind.

It would be a mistake to try to eliminate these conflicts. Clearly, it would be a mistake simply to eradicate an important part of one's cultural identity, to erase an important part of one's past, to refuse to empathize with other people, to avoid taking the long view, or to renounce the contributions of fantasy. Each side of these conflicts reveals different truths and enriches our lives; so even if it were possible to eradicate one of the opposed perspectives, doing so would impoverish our lives. It would also be a mistake to try to eliminate these conflicts by insisting on a compromise. The person who is both philosopher and poet should not avoid the inner conflict by becoming something "in between". Memories of our past selves should not prompt us to regress to a self that existed sometime between childhood and the present. Likewise, it would be a mistake to always empathize a little but not too much, to forgo narrow and wide perspectives in favor of an outlook that stayed in the mid-range, or to blend fantasy and reality into something sort-of-real. We ought also to be skeptical of attempts to eliminate these types of inner conflict through the introduction of some third, more encompassing alternative. Such alternatives tend to be overly abstract, eliminating the conflict by retreating from its details. Being a "seer" may sound like a good way to overcome the conflict between being a philosopher and being a poet, but it doesn't resolve anything in actual practice. Similarly, aspiring to a "timeless" self, or a greater sort of "caring", or a more "creative understanding" of reality may sound like routes to wholeness, but they are mostly empty promises. If we are honest with ourselves, we are stuck with several fundamental sorts of double consciousness.

Accepting inner conflict should mean more than just tolerating it. Being of two minds can be something that we value, and something that is deepening despite its discomforts. Juggling suggests one model for embracing double consciousness – a model that is particularly appropriate for the retention of multiple cultural identities. Isometrics offers another model – one in which opposing forces strengthen each other and together provide greater stability, and it is especially promising for the case of holding wide and narrow perspectives simultaneously. A third model, more relevant to the double consciousness produced by some cases of temporal doubling, is the model of the disruptor who continually counters our tendency towards amnesia and complacency. Being of two minds is not only okay, it is an important and positive part of being fully human.

# Addendum

Organizing our experience in accordance with more than one schema at a time enables us to be sensitive to more than one type of pattern at a time: one frame of mind highlights our shortcomings while another highlights our accomplishments, one economic theory focuses on inequities while another focuses on innovations, and so on. The resulting states of double consciousness are not always sustainable, of course, nor are they always desirable. This book has defended the desirability of *some* states of double consciousness without claiming that double consciousness is *always* a good thing. Although a full discussion of undesirable states of double consciousness would require another book, here I give some indication of situations where it is *not* okay to be of two minds.

The most obvious situation in which double consciousness should not be retained is one where the inner conflict is simply too painful. Models of juggling, of isometrics, and of purposeful disruption have pointed towards some promising ways of living with, indeed thriving with, inner conflict. But not everyone can avail themselves of these models at all times. And there is no guarantee that following these models will alleviate the suffering that comes with some inner conflicts. A child who experiences her parent as a loving caretaker but also as a dangerous abuser may find the combination of perspectives intolerably painful, and will need to abandon one perspective or the other in order to escape the trauma. (Multiple personality disorders can result from a person's inability to live with irreconcilable perspectives, and successful treatment of multiple personality disorders sometimes requires abandoning one or more personalities.) On the assumption that each perspective is revealing of some truths, simply abandoning one or the other will result in the loss of certain insights and certain forms of knowledge. Still, turning one's back on some forms of knowledge may be a necessary part of coping with a difficult situation.

There is no simple way to determine the amount of psychological pain one ought to tolerate for the sake of fuller insight. A soldier may find it extremely painful to view his opponents as vulnerable humans as well as efficient killers, but retaining both perspectives remains important, and tolerating the resulting pain is a large part of a soldier's challenge. The amount of psychological pain that an individual can tolerate also varies by age, by duration, and by situation. Older people tend to be more accepting of psychological pain, recognizing that it is a normal part of human life. Everyone finds pain more bearable if it is short-lived, knowing the end is in sight. Pain due to societal injustices, or evil intentions, is always harder to tolerate than pain due to one's own choices. For all of us, though, there are bound to be some states of double consciousness where alleviating the associated pain is more important than retaining the associated knowledge.

A second situation in which double consciousness should not be retained is one where the combination is paralyzing – where one's loyalty to conflicting viewpoints renders one unable to act on either. Faced with conflicting aims, conflicting advantages, we are not usually in the position of Buridan's ass, who dies because he is unable to choose between two different food choices. Conflicting options are seldom this evenly matched, and even if each of two options is equally acceptable, we are usually able to make a choice when a choice (arbitrary as it may be) must be made. Sometimes, however, recognizing the validity of a conflicting view – even if that view is less compelling – can incapacitate us. Viewing a surgical procedure as dangerous while also viewing it as life-saving – even if the chances favor its success – can keep one from making any decision at all (even if the effect of no decision is the same as choosing against surgery). Likewise, viewing a lucrative job offer as appealing while also viewing it as morally compromising can keep one from making a decision even if one thinks the moral view is more important (which can result in taking the job or not, depending on the circumstances). In situations where clear decisions and effective action are important, then, it may not be okay to be of two minds; despite the validity of a competing view, it may be best to put it out of mind.

States of paralysis are not always bad, and it is not always necessary to act on one's preferences. If we are equally drawn to the outlooks of competing politicians, it may be better to abstain from voting for either; and even if we find the view of one somewhat more compelling than the view of the other, the apparent validity of the competing view may recommend withholding one's vote altogether. Similarly, if we are of two minds about how to best help a friend – to stage an intervention or to support their bad choice, for example, it may be better to do nothing. There is a sense, of course, in which doing nothing is itself doing something; it has consequences for which we might bear some responsibility. Our knowledge of consequences is always limited, though, and, despite the arguments of some philosophers, most of us hold ourselves to be more responsible for the consequences of our actions than our inactions. So paralysis does not always rule against being of two minds.

A third, and less obvious situation where it is not okay to be of two minds is a situation where the retention of competing frameworks prevents either framework from evolving as it should in the face of further experience. If we regard the conflicting alternatives as enemies, each at war for their own self-preservation, then double consciousness can cause each frame of mind to become ever more rigid in the face of the opposition, denying its own weaknesses and resisting all concessions. The result is a kind of inner paralysis (much like the paralysis of some oppositional politics) that blocks the possibility of cognitive and emotional growth. If we are unable to relinquish a defensive stance on the part of competing frames of mind, it may be best to abandon one in order to develop a more responsive version of the other. In many cases, however, the competing perspectives of a double consciousness can help each other to be more responsive to new evidence. Continuing to hear a piece of music through the schema of G major and through the schema of E minor, or through the schema of tonal music and through the schema of atonal music, can help to highlight the anomalies within each framework in a way that leads to further refinement of each schematization. Continuing to view an addict as helpless and viewing him as making reasonable choices can help both views to evolve in the face of new observations as it keeps one aware of alternative ways of framing the available evidence and it prompts one to make appropriate modifications to that schema. (This was a feature of the isometrics model advocated throughout the book.)

Some outlooks or conceptual schemas are, by their very nature, so far removed from the evidence of one's senses as to be immune to the challenges of perceptual evidence. The view that everything is conscious and the opposing view that consciousness is just a myth are like this; nothing that we can point to could dislodge either view. (The panpsychist already knows that stones don't talk, and the eliminativist already knows what it is like to see the color red.) When double consciousness relies on these sorts of schemas, neither point of view is likely to change in response to any new input from the world. This does not render them invalid. They might still serve to highlight some interesting aspects of the world. And schemas for organizing our experience can be useful for things other than gaining knowledge of the world: they can improve the way that we interact with that world. Viewing everything as conscious might make us more respectful of our surroundings, for example, and viewing consciousness as a myth might force us to be more precise in our descriptions of people's minds. So, while an inability to evolve in the light of new evidence can count against particular outlooks as well as against particular states of double consciousness, such states can have other virtues that make them worth retaining.

# Notes

## INTRODUCTION

1 Elsewhere I have written about a variety of unconscious states, their power, and their limitations (Church, "Reasons of which Reason Knows Not", "The Hidden Image").

## QUARRELING WITH OURSELVES

1 It has been argued (Campbell) that Yeats, like Blake, thinks that poetry can achieve a mystical union of material contraries through the creation of a transcendent; but much of Yeats's poetry juxtaposes contraries without any attempt at their final union.
2 For an extended discussion of these themes in Shakespeare, see Greenblatt.
3 Emerson's and Eliot's notions of double consciousness are discussed in more detail by Rebekah Scott.
4 Schema theories became popular following Rumelhart; also Mandler. It is now common to see articles on spatial schemas, interpersonal schemas, reasoning schemas, and emotional schemas.
5 The reduction of knowledge to power has been particularly popular since Foucault's (1980) influential work on what he calls "power-knowledge".
6 The third "hat" that Piper wears is that of a practitioner of yoga, from whose perspective "the art and philosophy communities seem so preoccupied with chasing transient and illusionary goods that they seem simply to miss the basic point of being on the planet in the first place" (119).
7 Zizek (*The Parallax View*) pursues a similar comparison in his discussion of the Levi-Strauss example of two different maps of town (25).
8 This reason for quarrels is frequently cited in defense of adversarial legal systems: having different lawyers each making the strongest possible case for opposing points of view is justified on the grounds that it is the best way to bring all relevant facts to light – facts that can then be considered more impartially by either judge or jury. This line

of reasoning has been widely criticized, of course, on the grounds that competition is focused on winning rather than truth, and both juries and judges are easily manipulated by misleading ways of presenting the evidence.

9 In Chanter's words: "Neither object nor subject, the abject designates a domain to which those unthought, excluded others are relegated, whose borderline (non)existence secures the identity of those who occupy authoritative positions in relation to dominant discourses" (9).

10 This claim is developed in Davies and Egan.

11 The Hippocratic oath begins by specifying what *not* to do: "first do no ill". One might also insist: don't do anything for which you are unwilling to take responsibility. (Think about what this would mean in the domain of international aid, for example.)

12 Du Bois was heavily influenced by Hegel, who offered a series of third option resolutions of conflict. The German word "Aufhebung" has received seemingly contradictory translations (including "up-lifting", "sublation", "preservation", "abolishing", and "transcending") but Hegel's resolutions are clearly instances of supersessions according to the preceding taxonomy.

13 See Mullin for some further reflections on relevant divisions within and between individuals.

14 Another illustration of how a new type of music can emerge from the combination of conflicting genres can be found at Lam.

15 Some unavoidable conflicts, according to Freud (*Beyond the Pleasure Principle* and *Civilization and its Discontents*), result from tensions between the Pleasure Principle and the Reality Principle, Eros and Thanatos, or the Id and the Ego.

16 Anthony Atamanuik describes Donald Trump as his "Jungian shadow", "the part of me that I don't want the world to see, but that I'm showing all the time. . . . I want to have a relationship with that shadow, and understand it, as opposed to rejecting it" (Itzkoff). It is also known as one's "alter ego". Anne Sexton's therapist named Sexton's alter ego "Elizabeth", and recalled how "The focus of therapy as it pertained to Elizabeth was an effort to help Sexton recognize and tolerate the feelings she wanted to split off and act out" (Middlebrook 61).

17 Edith Spector Person offers detailed examples and analyses of such conflicts.

18 The trickster is said to play a similar role in some Native American lore and some Afro-Caribbean literature.

## TEMPORAL DOUBLING

1 John Locke considered memory to be the sole determinant of personal identity. He wrote: "For as far as any intelligent being can repeat the idea of any past action with the same consciousness it had of it at first, and

with the same consciousness it has of any present action; so far it is the
same personal self. For it is by the consciousness it has of its present
thoughts and actions, that it is self to itself now, and so will be the same
self, as far as the same consciousness can extend to actions past or to
come; and would be by distance of time, or change of substance, no
more two persons, than a man be two men by wearing other clothes
to-day than he did yesterday, with a long or a short sleep between: the
same consciousness uniting those distant actions into the same person,
whatever substances contributed to their production" (Book 2, Chap-
ter 27, sec 10). More recent neo-Lockeans often allow that there might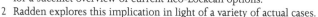
need to be physical as well as psychological continuity, and that psycho-
logical continuity may not require continuity of memory. See Tumulty
for a succinct overview of current neo-Lockean options.

2  Radden explores this implication in light of a variety of actual cases.

3  A good, up-to-date overview of these issues can be found in Tumulty.

4  Some degree of accuracy is needed in order for something to count as a
memory rather than a hallucination or a confabulation, but there is no
reason to think that so-called semantic memory is any more accurate
than so-called episodic memory. Some people are much better than
others at episodic recall ("hyperthymesia" is a term used for those who
have first-person recall of pretty much everything that has happened to
them); and some people are much better than others at semantic recall
(especially those who have made a regular practice of recounting their
life history).

5  About terms: Tulving and Donaldson attributed the term "semantic" memory to a 1966 doctoral dissertation by Quillian, and he proposed the contrasting term "episodic" memory (383). But, as he later
remarks, "The concept was first proposed some 30 years ago. . ., but
it has changed drastically since then and has now reached a stage at
which one can, as I am doing now, muse about it as a true marvel of
nature" ("Episodic Memory" 3). A further typological detail: Episodic
and semantic memory are usually cited as the two forms of explicit or
declarative memory, which is in turn contrasted with implicit or proce-
dural memory.

6  It seems that different parts of the brain are operative in the two types of
memory; also, that different types of memory have different behavioral
effects. For an overview of brain correlates, see Hart et al. and Head et al.

7  In Hadley's short story "The Abduction", the combination of past and
present perspectives is more volatile. It juxtaposes a teenager's entry into
the perspective of a hedonistic youth sub-culture with her later adop-
tion of the perspective of a "respectable" middle-class way of life – a
juxtaposition that, Hadley says, is "like a perfect experiment, testing one
version of the truth against another, incompatible version, and seeing
what explosions, what deformations result".

8 There is some question as to whether it counts as *imagining* (versus mere supposing) if it doesn't evoke any first-person perspective. Kung, on the other hand, wonders whether all imagining (versus hallucinating) must involve a semantic (he calls it "stipulative") element.

9 The fact that we have definitely had a past but may not have a future does add uncertainty to our future imaginings, but only to the imagined existence, not the imagined character, of that future. This asymmetry between memory and imaginative anticipation is relevant to rational planning, perhaps, but not to the phenomenology and ethics of inner conflict.

10 It is possible, however, to extend or refocus one's memory of a past outlook in such a way that one relives the past in a different (and still accurate) way. At least one therapeutic technique for dealing with trauma, EMDR (eye movement desensitization and reprocessing), takes this approach.

11 I think there is a limit on how indifferent to reason I could become and still be myself, but there are many disturbing possibilities short of a loss of self, or the replacement of one self with a new self. Piper ("Two Conceptions of the Self") defends, but overstates, the need for selves to be rational.

12 There is a trivial sense in which our present outlook includes our past outlooks – our past outlooks are included among the many causes of our present outlook; but causal relevance is not the same as contentful subsumption.

13 A recent example of this strategy can be found in a recent interview with Anthony Kronman, who says: "All of us have multiple beliefs. Say you believe in God. You also believe in other things: science, or the value of literature, or democracy. If you're a curious and reflective person, you'll be moved to ask: How do all these beliefs fit together? You could say, 'Well, I guess I'm an atheist, because only atheism will save my science, aesthetics, and politics.' Or you could say, 'It's God first and only, and if I have to throw those other things overboard, so be it.' . . . Or it could be that, by adjusting your conception of God, you could harmonize your beliefs, so that they fit together in an intellectually coherent and respectable way". Tillich's redefinition of "God" as "ultimate concern" also has this flavor.

14 Herder insists that greater understanding of the universe (by which he means scientific understanding) adds to our sense of the sublime – in opposition to Kant, for whom an experience of the sublime is an experience of something that we recognize as existing beyond the reach of our understanding (not just our actual understanding but our possible understanding). See Zuckert.

15 Some of the costs of such a view are detailed in Radden, Chapter 12, "The Normative Tug of Individualism". Although she disagrees with

Kantians like Korsgaard, who find this view unintelligible, she thinks the moral, emotional, and epistemic costs are prohibitive.

16 The logical contradiction is addressed by David Lewis ("Counterparts of Persons and Their Bodies", "Survival and Identity"), writing about time slices.

17 This is an important theme in the work of Soteriou, who distinguishes memory and imagination from perception by appeal to the different intentions or aims that guide our experience of each. On the other hand, Richard Wollheim, Chapter IV, emphasizes the transferred motivational force of what he calls "iconic" or "experiential" memories.

18 Ludwig Wittgenstein is famous for his attempt to trace experiential knots to linguistic knots, and his attempt to disentangle the former by disentangling the latter. Insofar as that strategy depends on keeping various language "games" separate, one might wonder about the extent to which such separation is psychologically possible.

19 The poet-speaker she refers to is Ted Hughes, whose "poem is about a single exposure, but the single exposure is our exposure, as we find for ourselves, or are meant to find, in a shuddering awareness of death and life together" (21–22).

20 He contrasts this with so-called scholarly memory, or historic research, which runs counter to nostalgic memory.

21 There is a difference between unconscious *influences* and unconscious *memories* but the distinction isn't important here. I address this distinction further in Church ("Reasons of Which Reason Knows Not").

22 Freud (*Beyond the Pleasure Principle*) claims that the analyst's task is to help the patient to retain "some degree of aloofness which will enable him . . . to recognize that what appears to be reality is in fact only a reflection of a forgotten past". See also Wollheim, especially Chapter VIII, on "overcoming the past" without simply forgetting it.

23 Moran argues that occupying a first-person perspective on one's thoughts and actions is crucial for our ownership of (versus estrangement from) those thoughts and actions. Following in the footsteps of Sartre, he maintains that the avoidance of a first-person perspective is the avoidance of responsibility.

24 Such juggling complicates our experience in ways that are enlightening and enriching as well as taxing (though it is not clear that insisting on just one point of view is less taxing than allowing oneself to hold multiple points of view).

25 I am not claiming that past perspectives or dispositions ought always to be cultivated in the present, or that strengthening them will always add to one's overall balance and stability. Among other considerations is the fact that psychological balance doesn't always produce sociological balance.

26 I do not think Eliot saw it quite this way. For her, although Balstrode's past perspective of righteousness was problematic, it was preferable (in

some objective way) to his later self-serving pragmatism. In the opening quote of this chapter his shame about his present is "merited".

27 Sacks observes that "The hours and minutes still seem excruciatingly long when I am bored and all too short when I am engaged" (34). On the other hand, he reports the work of Christof Koch as suggesting that intense attention in the face of an emergency makes time seem to slow down (39).

## BRINGING THE OTHER WITHIN

1 According to most theories of childhood development, psychological separation from one's parent or primary caretaker is an early yet seldom completed process; its remnants continue to affect most adult relationships. People are autonomous to different degrees, depending in part on how well they were able to separate from their parents or other loved ones; and, of course, people can be more or less autonomous with respect to different aspects of their lives. For further discussion of what it means to internalize another person, see Church ("Morality and the Internalized Other").

2 For a fuller discussion of what it means to internalize a belief or an outlook see Church ("Taking It to Heart").

3 For further discussion of what it means to "own" one's actions, or to "own" one's body, see Church ("Taking It to Heart" and *Possibilities of Perception*).

4 The literature on self-deception addresses this sort of mismatch, as does some more recent literature on belief versus "alief". See Gendler.

5 I distinguish empathy from emotional (or cognitive) contagion, which can happen automatically. In the case of emotional contagion, one adopts rather than imagines the other's point of view.

6 "Everyone would think that what he was hearing now was just what he'd longed for all this time to come together and be fused with the one he loved and become one instead of two. The reason is that this is our original natural state and we used to be whole creatures: 'love' is the name for the desire and pursuit of wholeness" (Plato).

7 Freud also relates the melting away of a self/other boundary experienced "at the height of being in love" to the "oceanic" feeling that underlies certain religious sentiments – a connection echoed in Spector Person's comments, following.

8 "[T]he Lover wants to be 'the whole World' for the beloved . . . a this which includes all other thises. . . . [I]f the beloved is transformed into an automaton, the lover finds himself alone. Thus the lover does not desire to possess the beloved as one possesses a thing; he demands a special type of appropriation. He wants to possess a freedom as freedom" (Sartre 367).

9 Exceptions include cases where the internalized other is an abusive parent, or where the internalized other is a charismatic but seriously deluded teacher.

10 More direct forms of empathy might result from simply mimicking or absorbing the emotions we perceive in others. But this will not give us *knowledge* of another's state of mind unless and until we imagine that the state we are experiencing is also the state they are experiencing.

11 The term "theory" is used rather loosely here – to include idiosyncratic suppositions about a particular individual as well as broadly supported generalizations about human behavior.

12 See Stich and Nichols for a detailed sorting out of this debate. It now seems fair to say that our understanding of others is underwritten by both theory and simulation (assuming that both can occur without consciousness).

13 The German "kennen" versus "verstehen", and the Spanish "conocer" versus "entender", mark such a contrast.

14 Even on a Kantian conception of morality, where intentions must be directed by a rational will rather than by feeling (and where it is easier to know that one's intentions are the result of a rational will if they run counter to one's feelings), empathy can be important as a way to draw our attention to things we need to consider in formulating our intentions.

15 Simon Blackburn (in Antony) defends his unwillingness to participate in a religious ritual at a friend's home on the grounds that his host's invitation disregards his conflicting beliefs. There is an apparent blindness, however, to the distinction between deferring to another in one's actions and deferring to another in one's beliefs.

## NARROW AND WIDE PERSPECTIVES

1 In his essay "The Absurd" (*Mortal Questions* 11–23) and in *The View from Nowhere* (1986) the contrast seems merely epistemic – a difference between two ways of knowing. In "What it is Like to Be a Bat" and "Brain Bisection and the Unity of Consciousness" (*Mortal Questions* 165–180, 147–164, respectively), the contrast appears to be metaphysical as well – a difference between two aspects of reality.

2 See, especially, Chapter XI, "Solipsism, Dissociation, and the Impersonal Standpoint".

3 I do not equate subjective versus objective with narrower versus wider, but Nagel's essay on the latter is included in a collection dedicated to the former and there is considerable overlap in his views about each.

4 We can certainly have the *thought* that there are no meanings and no evaluations independent of our narrower, human perspective, but we can't

adopt a point of view (even in imagination) without categorizing our experience in some way and thereby attributing meanings and values of some sort. Nagel (*The View from Nowhere*) acknowledges this impossibility.

5  I am less convinced by his rejection of "middle ground" solutions in the case of alien beings. Imagination can take us far with respect to a bat – as he himself seems to acknowledge in a footnote (*Mortal Questions* 172).

6  Subsumptions could work in the opposite direction as well – as an idealist subsumes the objective under the subjective. With respect to subjective versus objective perspectives on psychological states, Nagel entertains the possibility of a third option which would supersede both subjective and objective – what he calls an "objective phenomenology" (*The Possibility of Altruism* 178–180); this is an elusive notion but it is even harder to imagine a third option that supersedes both narrow and wide, and both important and unimportant.

7  There are some cases where adopting a broader perspective can help one to count a large number of objects because it enables one to group things more efficiently, and widening one's perspective can also perform a delicate task such as threading a needle because it steadies one's hand, for example; but these are not cases of significant widening and they are not cases of doubling one's perspective.

8  Perception, insofar as it informs action, must register subjective location in space and time; language is, by definition, more universal. But, of course, there may be more abstract forms of perception (the perception of numbers, for example), and more idiosyncratic forms of language (a secret language of siblings, for example).

9  Note that this is not the same as claiming that science requires one to adhere to objectivity; some science is very local, and some science is well served by infusions of subjectivity (empathy with animals, and perhaps with plants, for example).

10  A useful explication of this analysis can be found in Simpson (2008).

11  Rothman bemoans U2's move away from its ironic stance, which may be part of a larger movement within the arts. Recent writing by Edward St. Aubyn (*The Patrick Melrose Novels*) and by David Foster Wallace (*Infinite Jest*), for example, have launched pointed attacks on the culture of irony.

12  Note that another's claims are not automatically justified from their perspective since standards internal to a particular vocabulary can discredit the beliefs of those using that vocabulary.

13  Moody-Adams points out that the practical philosopher must engage with society, which requires her to be openly critical of others; keeping one's criticisms private, or dissimulating with universalist language that one doesn't really believe is not really an option. Young argues that Rorty's strategy for increasing human solidarity "in fact undermines the solidarity of community and reinforces the status quo". Moody-Adams also highlights an apparent contradiction in Rorty's own stance

whereby he suggests that irony is a private matter yet promotes it as a public intellectual. Young notes the apparent contradiction between Rorty's derisive remarks about his "metaphysician" opponent and his stated commitment to use more inclusive language in order to avoid humiliation.

14 Brookner describes the ironic stance of a character as follows: "This was a state over which irony ruled, a mocking acquiescence totally divorced from the reality of desire . . . a distant contempt" (162). In a similar vein, Lear notes that "What is peculiar to irony is its undermining of a passion or motivation – the way it brings action to a halt" (19). (This is in contrast to his claim that "ironic existence does not require alienation from established social practice . . . is compatible with passionate engagement in social life" (30).)

15 Such humor is just one instance of a wider class of incongruities that tend to provoke laughter.

16 I am using the term "hysterical" as understood colloquially; its status as a diagnostic category is largely outdated. Note, too, that the views that I am calling more "objective" views may or may not be equated with socially dominant views.

17 With regard to laughter, Sass maintains that "No one who has interviewed schizophrenics will have failed, at times, to have the sneaking suspicion that the whole interaction is, to the patient, something of a joke" (112).

18 The passage is prompted by Lydgate's impulse to propose marriage: "he was bent on telling her that he adored her, and on asking her to marry him. He knew that this was like the sudden impulse of a madman – incongruous even with his habitual foibles. No matter! It was the one thing which he was resolved to do. He had two selves within him apparently, and they must learn to accommodate each other and bear reciprocal impediments. Strange, that some of us, with quick alternate vision, see beyond our infatuations, and even while we rave on the heights, behold the wide plain where our persistent self pauses and awaits us" (chapter XV).

19 In some cases, the more emotional state is the one with the broader view. A nice example of this can be found in Sittenfeld: "being deeply upset didn't preclude my remarking on his syntax" (64).

20 Carnival humor often depends on effecting this inversion. See Stallybrass and White.

21 A nice example of this strategy with respect to the low versus high is described in Litvak. What Litvak admires about Proust is his ability to focus on the "high" in a way that feeds the pleasures of the low – something that he achieves by analyzing the various idiocies and pretensions of high society (and intellectualism, and adulthood more generally) in such a way that the analyses themselves become a source

of fresh pleasure. The elaborately disguised maneuvering of high society is exposed in minute detail, and the relishing of these details replaces one's initial, naïve fascination with a more sophisticated but equally uninhibited enjoyment. Rather than indulging in high-minded oversight of the low – a stance that tends to destroy immediacy and enthusiasm, we can pursue low-minded analyses of the high – an activity that provides new surprises and pleasures.

22 Roy Perrett suggests: "The *Gita's* advice is to concentrate exclusively on the performance of the duties attendant on our communal roles and, in doing so, to surrender all attachment to the fruits of our action" (33).

23 There are some parallels between this alternative to Nagel regarding a wide view and Herder's alternative to Kant regarding the sublime. See Zuckert.

24 A good, accessible example of this is Galeano.

## LIVING AS IF

1 Note the similarity to a more famous quote by Mahatma Gandhi (who was born more than 50 years later, in 1869): "Live as if you were to die tomorrow. Learn as if you were to live forever". Earlier sources of the quote may include Isidore of Seville (c. 560–636) in his *Etymologiae*, and Edmund Rich (1175–1240) as cited in *American Journal of Education* (1877). In the *Hitopadesha* (a collection of Sanskrit fables from a thousand years ago), verse 3 has a version of the same idea: "A wise person should think about knowledge and wealth as though never ageing or dying, but should act according to dharma as though death had already grabbed him by the hair".

2 One might describe the case of avoidance as a special kind of pretense – namely, the pretense of an absence; but I am reserving the notion of pretense for mental actions that involve the creation of new content rather than the erasure of old. Likewise, one might describe the imagining of something false the creation of an illusion, but "illusion" suggests "delusion" and I am not talking about states in which one is misled into believing something false.

3 Following Kant, one might insist that thoughts (or words) are empty unless and until they are translated into spatiotemporal experiences, which is precisely what the imagination does. I am sympathetic to this argument (Church, *Possibilities of Perception*), but what I am claiming here is considerably weaker: I am not claiming that thoughts are meaningless apart from the involvement of imagination, only that they cannot support the relevant "as if" experiences without the involvement of the imagination. Also, I am not claiming that all imagining requires spatiotemporal images, only that imagining something requires us to conjure up/imitate/recreate some experience of that thing.

4 The possible value of living as if there were a god overseeing our lives is a familiar theme – nicely expressed in these lines from a poem by Idea Vilariño: "open the hand and give me / the dirty dirty crumb/as if a god as if the wind / as if the hand that opens / that distracts destiny / were granting us a day".

5 A clear case of this latter alternative might be the atheist who, wanting to believe in the presence of a benevolent power, limits her interactions and her reflections in an attempt to revise her beliefs accordingly. Less clear cases include the lover who tries to discount evidence of her partner's disloyalty, and the case of the applicant who tries to convince herself that she is the best person for a job. See Church ("Taking It to Heart") for my views on when it is, and when it is not, possible to choose one's beliefs.

6 "And the stars, / Surely the stars too, shake with laughter" (Hughes 192).

7 Consider Ariela Lazar's description of self-deceptive states: "whereas a simple daydream exerts a rather restricted influence on one's choices and thinking, the self-deceptive state affects one's behavior no differently than most beliefs: it figures in both practical and theoretical reasoning. . . . States of self-deception are a sort of hybrid: they are strongly influenced by desires and emotions – they express them – yet they inform our behavior more or less in the way that beliefs do. We need not be puzzled on encountering a state which functions much like a belief does even though its content primarily corresponds to a desire. A great number of beliefs deviate from norms of rational belief formation" (286). Lazar presents self-deceptive states as states that have the rational effects of beliefs without having the rational causes of beliefs; but, as she then acknowledges, many beliefs fail to have fully rational causes or fully rational effects.

8 Assuming that knowledge entails belief, the claim that one knows something to be a falsehood may seem to beg that question against the suggestion that one might nonetheless believe it. But I think it is possible to hold contradictory beliefs and, in any case, the same point could be made by claiming that *asserts* or *maintains*, as opposed to *knows*, that it is false.

9 As Horwich points out, there is no real distinction within science between instrumentally true and actually true if there is no competing view of what is true.

10 Something similar could be said of physicists relying on Newtonian physics for many calculations despite knowing that Newtonian physics has been displaced by relativity theory. In this case, however, Newtonian physics simplifies rather than diverges from the truth; it serves as a useful approximation of the truth (much as saying that I am swimming in $H_2O$, versus a mix of $H_2O$ and $Na^+$ and $Cl^-$ and several other ions, can serve as a useful approximation of the truth). This is also the case with

so-called "folk psychology", according to which people act on the basis of rational combinations of beliefs and desires. See Appiah's defense of the intentional stance and of decision theory as useful idealizations.

11 It might be said that *all* representations of numbers are misleading in some way, and that it is only a question of what sorts of misleading are more problematic in what contexts. I am sympathetic to this claim; the same point can be made by considering the shift from linguistic representations to graphic representations.

12 The capacity to be precise in this way might be because of the fact that numbers have (indeed, are defined by) just one kind of property (quantity) while most things in the world have many different kinds of properties (colors, textures, sizes, durations, etc.).

13 One of Descartes's great insights was the fact that any algebraic relation could be represented as a geometrical relation – something that he realized could be extremely helpful in attempting to "intuit" mathematical truths. See Church ("Boundary Problems"), Chapter III, for further discussion of the relevance of this discovery to the possibility of perceptual knowledge of mathematical truths.

14 There is also a growing countercurrent, of course, especially among those who reject their assigned gender, that insists on the intrinsic, inescapable character of one's gender identity.

15 Hegel is a large part of Butler's background and inspiration, so it is no surprise that she is especially attuned to the positive potential of perspectival conflict.

16 There are many different ways that such a construction may be brought about – some involving alterations in the physical world, some not. See Church ("Making Order out of Disorder").

17 This position is defended by Smilansky, for example. A nice overview of related positions can be found in Caruso. Most arguments against the reality of free will stem from a commitment to determinism and the conviction that free will is incompatible with determinism. Other reasons for denying the existence of free will include the large role that chance plays in our lives. For that argument, see Levy.

18 See Church ("Boundary Problems"), Chapter III, for a defense of the possibility of perceiving causal relations. I do not reject the possibility of perceiving any absence – an absence of elephants, or an absence of the color red, for example – only the possibility of perceiving (and thus imagining in a sensory way) the absence of a counterfactual dependency.

19 This interest dovetails with a growing interest in the benefits of living as if there were a god even though one believes there is not. See Antony, and Johnston. Richard Rorty discusses the advantages of the masses assuming that their values are objective, and he discusses the rather different advantages of the elite recognizing that values are not objective (see Chapter 4). Rorty does not, however, recommend that either

group live *as if* values were objective; this would require an undesirable self-consciousness on the part of the masses, and it would impair the elite's efforts at creative reinterpretation.

20 The "projectivist" position, which is also called "quasi-realist", was articulated by Simon Blackburn and later applied more fully to the case of ethical values by Alan Gibbard, for example.

21 The analogy between a property of goodness and a property of redness is G.E. Moore (*Principia Ethica*). Moore, however, believed that both goodness and redness were in fact simple intrinsic properties. There are other ways to understand, or to imagine, the objectivity of values. Here I focus on just one, relatively simple way.

22 Nagel's "Brain Bisection and the Unity of Consciousness" (in *Mortal Questions*) presents the argument against the reality of a unified consciousness and only briefly discusses the importance of this illusion for empathy. That importance is discussed more fully in his *The Possibility of Altruism*.

23 I am aware that the fantasy of a point self may also encourage us to think of people as totally unpredictable insofar as points are unconstrained by any internal structure. Viewed in this way, the fantasy of a point self becomes much like the fantasy of a free will (as discussed earlier) – probably too "empty" to guide any meaningful sort of "as if" living.

# Works Cited

Antony, Louise M. *Philosophers Without Gods*. Oxford UP, 2007.

Anzaldua, Gloria. *Borderlands/La Frontera: The New Mestiza*. Aunt Lute Books, 1987.

Appiah, Kwame Anthony. *As If: Idealizations and Ideals*. Harvard UP, 2017.

Armstrong, Paul B. "Henry James and Neuroscience: Cognitive Universals and Cultural Differences." *The Henry James Review*, vol. 39, no. 2, 2018, pp. 133–151.

Bakhtin, M.M. *Speech Genres and Other Late Essays*. U of Texas P, 1986.

Bayne, Tim, and David Chalmers. "What Is the Unity of Consciousness?" *The Unity of Consciousness*, edited by Alex Cleeremans, Oxford UP, 2003.

Blackburn, Simon. *Spreading the Word*. Oxford UP, 1984.

Bloom, Paul. *Against Empathy: The Case for Rational Compassion*. Ecco, 2016.

Breton, André. *Manifesto of Surrealism*. 1924.

———. "Évolution du concept de la liberté," cited by Maria Clara Bernal, "André Breton's Anthology of Freedom: The Contagious Power of Revolt." *Surrealism in Latin America: Vivisimo Muerto*, edited by Dawn Ades, et al., Tate Publishing in Association with the Getty Research Institute, 2012, p. 1.

Brookner, Anita. *Making Things Better*. Vintage, 2004.

Burton, Krista. "The Astrology Cure." *The New York Times Sunday Review*, June 17, 2018, p. 2.

Butler, Judith. *Subjects of Desire: Hegelian Reflections in Twentieth Century*. Columbia UP, 1987.

———. *Gender Trouble: Feminism and the Subversion of Identity*. Routledge, 1990.

Campbell, Michael. "Blake's System of Contraries as a Terrible Beauty." *Dialogue*, Apr. 1988.

Caruso, Gregg D. "Free Will Eliminativism: Reference, Error, and Phenomenology." *Philosophical Studies*, vol. 172, no. 10, 2015, pp. 2823–2833.

Chabon, Michael. "The True Meaning of Nostalgia." *The New Yorker*, Mar. 25, 2017.

Chang, Ruth. "How to Make Hard Choices." 2014. www.ted.com/talks/ruth_chang_how_to_make_hard_choices.

Chanter, Tina. *The Picture of Abjection: Film, Fetish, and the Nature of Difference.* Indiana UP, 2008.

Church, Jennifer. "Morality and the Internalized Other." *The Cambridge Companion to Freud*, edited by Jerome Neu, Cambridge Press, 1991, pp. 209–223.

———. "Ownership and the Body." *Feminists Rethink the Self*, edited by Diana Meyers, Westview Press, 1997, pp. 85–104.

———. "Taking It to Heart: What Choice Do We Have?" *Monist*, vol. 85, no. 3, 2002, pp. 205–221.

———. "Making Order out of Disorder: On the Social Construction of Madness." *The Philosophy of Psychiatry: A Companion*, edited by Jennifer Radden, Oxford UP, 2004, pp. 393–407.

———. "Reasons of which Reason Knows Not." *Philosophy, Psychiatry, and Psychology*, vol. 12, no. 1, 2005, pp. 31–41.

———. "The Hidden Image: A Defense of Unconscious Imagining and its Importance." *American Imago*, vol. 65, no. 3, 2008, pp. 379–404.

———. *Possibilities of Perception*. Oxford UP, 2013.

———. "Boundary Problems: Negotiating the Challenges of Responsibility and Loss." *Oxford Handbook of the Philosophy of Psychiatry*, edited by K.W.M. Fulford, et al., Oxford UP, 2013, pp. 497–511.

Dames, Nicholas. *Amnesiac Selves: Nostalgia, Forgetting, and British Fiction 1810–1870.* Oxford UP, 2001.

Davies, Martin and Egan, Francis. "Delusion, Cognitive Approaches: Bayesian Inference and Compartmentalization." *The Oxford Handbook of Philosophy and Psychiatry*, edited by K.W.M. Fulford, et al., Oxford UP, 2013, pp. 689–727.

Deleuze, Gilles. *Foucault.* Translated by S. Hand. U of Minnesota P, 1988.

———. *The Fold: Leibniz and the Baroque.* U of Minnesota P, 1992.

Deleuze, Gilles and Guatarri, Felix. *A Thousand Plateaus: Capitalism and Schizophrenia.* U of Minnesota P, 1987.

Derrida, Jacques. *Of Grammatology.* Translated by Gayatri Chakravorty Spivak. Les Editions de Minuit, 1976; Johns Hopkins UP, 1998.

———. *On Cosmopolitanism and Forgiveness.* Routledge, 2001.

Diamond, Cora. "The Difficulty of Reality and the Difficulty of Philosophy." *Partial Answers: Journal of Literature and the History of Ideas*, vol. 1, no. 2, 2003, pp. 1–26.

Donath, Orna. *Regretting Motherhood: A Study.* North Atlantic Books, 2017.

Du Bois, W.E.B. *The Souls of Black Folk.* Penguin Press, 1989/1903.

Eagleton, Terry. "Not Just Anybody." *London Review of Books*, Jan. 5, 2017.

Eliot, George. *Middlemarch.* Wordsworth Editions Ltd, 1998/1871–2.

———. "The Lifted Veil." *'The Lifted Veil' and 'Brother Jacob'*, edited by Helen Small, Oxford UP, 1999/1859, pp. 1–44.

**Why It's OK** to Be of Two Minds

Emerson, Ralph Waldo. "The Transcendentalist: A Lecture Given at the Masonic Temple, Boston, 1942." *Emerson on Transcendentalism*, edited by Edward L. Erickson, Edward L. Ungar Press, 1987, pp. 91–109.

Foucault, Michel. *Power/Knowledge: Selected Interviews*. Vintage, 1980.

———. *Madness and Civilization: A History of Insanity in the Age of Reason*. Vintage, 1988.

Frankfurt, Harry. *The Reasons of Love*. Princeton UP, 2006.

Freud, Sigmund. *Beyond the Pleasure Principle*. W.W. Norton and Company, 1980/1920.

———. *Civilization and its Discontents*. W.W. Norton and Company, 2010/1930.

Galeano, Edwardo. *Open Veins of Latin America: Five Centuries of the Pillage of a Continent*. Monthly Review Press, 1997/1971.

Gendler, Tamara. "Belief and Alief." *Contemporary Epistemology: An Anthology*, edited by Jeremy Fantl, et al, John Wiley and Sons, 2019.

Gibbard, Alan. *Wise Choices, Apt Feelings: A Theory of Normative Judgement*. Harvard UP, 1990.

Gopnik, Adam. "Trollope Trending." *The New Yorker*, May 4, 2015, pp. 28–32.

Greenblatt, Stephen. *Will in the World: How Shakespeare Became Shakespeare*. W.W. Norton and Company, 2004.

Greenspan, Patricia. "A Case of Mixed Feelings: Ambivalence and the Logic of Emotion." *Explaining Emotions*, edited by A.O. Rorty, U of California P, 1980, pp. 223–250.

Hadley, Tessa. "An Abduction. Including interview with Deborah Treisman." *The New Yorker*, June 9, 2012.

———. "Return to 'The Secret Garden'". The New Yorker Jun 6 & 13, 2016.

Hart, John, Jr. et al. "Neural Substrates of Semantic Memory." *Journal of the International Neuropsychological Society*, vol. 13, no. 5, 2007, pp. 865–880.

Head, Denise, et al. "Neuroanatomical and Cognitive Mediators of Age-Related Differences in Episodic Memory." *Neuropsychology*, vol. 22, no. 4, 2008, pp. 491–507.

Hegel, G.W.F. *The Phenomenology of Spirit*. Oxford UP, 1977/1807.

Horwich, Paul. *From a Deflationary Point of View*. Oxford UP, 2004.

Hughes, Ted. "Freedom of Speech." *Birthday Letters*. Farrar, Straus and Giroux, 1989.

Hurley, Susan. *Consciousness in Action*. Harvard UP, 1998.

Itzkoff, Dave. "Trump Becomes a Late-Night Host." *New York Times*, Apr. 24, 2017, p. C6.

Johnston, Mark. *Saving God: Religion after Idolatry*. Princeton UP, 2009.

Kahneman, Daniel. *Thinking, Fast and Slow*. Farrar, Straus and Giroux, 2011.

Kant, Immanuel. *Critique of Pure Reason*. Macmillan, 1929/1787.

Knausgaard, Karl Ove. *My Struggle: Books 1–6*. Farrar, Straus and Giroux, 2013–2018.

Koch, Philip. "Emotional Ambivalence." *Philosophy and Phenomenological Research*, vol. 48, no. 2, 1987, pp. 257–279.

Korsgaard, Christine. *The Sources of Normativity*. Harvard, 1992.

Kronman, Anthony. *Confessions of a Born-Again Pagan*. Yale UP, 2016.

Kung, Peter. "Imagination as a Guide to Possibility." *Philosophy and Phenomenological Research*, vol. 81, no. 3, 2010, pp. 620–663.

Lam, Barry. https://hiphination.org/episodes/episode-5-the-cops-of-pop/ Feb 21, 2017.

Lau, Hakwan, and David M. Rosenthal. "Empirical Support for Higher-Order Theories of Conscious Awareness." *Trends in Cognitive Sciences*, edited by Miao-Kun Sun, Nova Science Pub Inc, 2011.

Lazar, Ariela. "Deceiving Oneself or Self-Deceived? On the Formation of Beliefs 'Under the Influence'." *Mind*, vol. 108, no. 430, 1999.

Lear, Jonathan. *A Case for Irony*. Harvard UP, 2011.

Leslie, A.M. "Pretense and Representation: The Origins of 'Theory of Mind'." *Psychological Review*, vol. 94, no. 4, 1987, pp. 412–26.

Levy, Neil. *Hard Luck: How Luck Undermines Free Will and Moral Responsibility*. Oxford UP, 2015.

Lewis, David. "Counterparts of Persons and Their Bodies." *Philosophical Papers*, Vol. I. Oxford UP, 1983.

———. "Survival and Identity." *Philosophical Papers*, Vol. I, Oxford UP, 1983.

Litvak, Joseph. "Strange Gourmet: Taste, Waste, Proust." *Novel Gazing: Queer Readings in Fiction*, edited by Eve Kosofsky Sedgwick, Duke UP, 1997.

Locke, John. *An Essay Concerning Human Understanding*. Penguin Classics, 1998/1689.

Maibom, Heidi. "Feeling for Others: Empathy, Sympathy, and Morality." *Inquiry*, vol. 52, no. 5, 2009, pp. 483–499.

Mandler, J.M. *Stories, Scripts, and Scenes: Aspects of Schema Theory*. Lawrence Erlbaum Associates, 1984.

McDowell, John. *Mind and World*. Harvard UP, 1994.

Meltzer, Francoise. *Seeing Double: Baudelaire's Modernity*. U of Chicago P, 2011.

Middlebrook, Diane Wood. *Anne Sexton: A Biography*. Vintage, 1992.

Mill, John Stuart. *On Liberty*. The Walter Scott Publishing Company, 2011/1859.

Millhauser, Steven. "Clair de Lune." *The Knife Thrower and Other Stories*. Vintage, 1998.

Mitchell, Maria. www.brainyquote.com/authors/maria_mitchell

Moody-Adams, Michele M. "Theory, Practice, and the Contingency of Rorty's Irony." *Journal of Social Philosophy*, 25th Anniversary Special Issue, 1994, pp. 209–227.

Moore, G.E. *Principia Ethica*. Dover Publications, 2004/1903.

Moore, Lorrie. "Community Life." *The New Yorker*, Sept. 30, 1991, pp. 29–36.

Moran, Richard. *Authority and Estrangement: An Essay on Self-Knowledge.* Princeton UP, 2001.

Mullin, Amy. "Selves, Diverse and Divided: Can Feminists Have Diversity without Multiplicity?" *Hypatia*, vol. 10, no. 4, 1995, pp. 1–31.

Nagel, Thomas. *The Possibility of Altruism.* Princeton UP, 1979.

———. *Mortal Questions.* Cambridge UP, 1979.

———. *The View from Nowhere.* Oxford UP, 1986.

Nietzsche, Friedrich. *Beyond Good and Evil: Prelude to a Philosophy of the Future.* Dover Publications, 1997/1886.

———. *A Genealogy of Morals.* Oxford UP, 2009/1886.

———. *Truth and Lies in a Non-Moral Sense.* CreateSpace Independent Publishing Platform, 2015/1896.

Parfit, Derek. *Reasons and Persons.* Oxford UP, 1984.

Paul, L.A. *Transformative Experience.* Oxford UP, 2014.

Paz, Octavio. *Corrienta Alterna/Alternating Current.* Translated by Helen R. Lane and Helen R. Wildwood House, 1967/1974.

Pence Fritsch, Nancy. "The President Pence Delusion." (interview with Jane Mayer) *The New Yorker*, Oct. 23, 2017.

Perrett, Roy W. *An Introduction to Indian Philosophy.* Cambridge UP, 2016.

Piper, Adrian. "Two Conceptions of the Self." *Philosophical Studies*, vol. 48, 1985, pp. 173–197.

———. "Impartiality, Compassion, and Modal Imagination." *Ethics*, vol. 101, no. 4, 1991, pp. 726–757.

———. "Passing for White, Passing for Black." *Transition*, vol. 58, 1992, pp. 4–32.

———. "On Wearing Three Hats." *Adrian Piper Research Archive*, 2007/1996, pp. 117–127.

Plato. *Symposium.*

Plessner, Helmuth. *Laughing and Crying: A Study of the Limits of Human Behavior.* Translated by James Spencer and Marjorie Greene. Northwestern, 1970.

Proust, Marcel. *Le Temps retrouvé/Remembrance of Things Past.* Vintage, 1982/1913–27.

Radden, Jennifer. *Divided Minds and Successive Selves: Ethical Issues in Disorders of Identity and Personality.* MIT Press, 1996.

Rorty, Amelie. "A Plea for Ambivalence." *OUP Handbook of Philosophy of Education*, edited by Peter Goldie, Oxford UP, 2010.

Rorty, Richard. "Private Irony and Liberal Hope." *Contingency, Irony, and Solidarity.* Cambridge UP, 1989.

Rothman, Joshua. "Bring Back the Irony." *The New Yorker*, July 31, 2015.

Rovane, Carol. *The Bounds of Agency: An Essay in Revisionary Metaphysics*. Princeton UP, 1998.

———. "Does Rationality Enforce Identity?" *Self and Self-Knowledge*, edited by A. Coliva, Oxford UP, 2012.

Rumelhart, D.E. "Schemata: The Building Blocks of Cognition." *Theoretical Issues in Reading Comprehension*, edited by R.J. Spiro, et al., Lawrence Erlbaum, 1980.

Rutledge, Dennis M. "Du Bois's Concept of Double Consciousness: Myth and Reality." *Research in Race & Ethnic Relations*, vol. 9, 1996, pp. 69–90.

Sacks, Oliver. *The River of Consciousness*. Knopf, 2017.

Sartre, Jean-Paul. *Being and Nothingness*. Translated by Hazel Barnes. Washington Square Press, 1993/1943.

Sass, Louis A. *Madness and Modernism: Insanity in the Light of Modern Art, Literature, and Thought*. Harvard UP, 1994.

Scott, Rebekah. "Indifferent Curiosity: 'Double Consciousness' and Oxymoron in *The Ambassadors*." *Henry James and the Poetics of Duplicity*, edited by Dennis Tredy, et al., Cambridge Scholars Publishing, 2013.

Siderits, Mark. *Personal Identity and Buddhist Philosophy: Empty Persons*. Routledge, 2003.

Simpson, David. "Irony, Dissociation and the Self." *Journal of Consciousness Studies*, vol. 15, no. 6, 2008, pp. 119–135.

Sittenfeld, Curtis. "Show Don't Tell." *The New Yorker*, June 5 &12, 2017.

Smilansky, Saul. *Free Will and Illusion*. Oxford UP, 2000.

Sölle, Dorothee. *Suffering*. Translated by Everett R. Kalin. Fortress Press, 1984.

Soteriou, Mathew. *The Mind's Construction*. Oxford UP, 2013.

Spector Person, Edith. *Dreams of Love and Fateful Encounters: The Power of Romantic Passion*. American Psychiatric Publications Inc, 2006.

Stallybrass, Peter, and Allon White. *The Politics and Poetics of Transgression*. Cornell UP, 1986.

Stephen Stich, Stephen and Nichols, Shaun. *Mindreading: An Integrated Account of Pretence, Self-Awareness, and Understanding Other Minds*. Oxford UP, 2003.

Strawson, Galen. "Against Narrative." *Arguing About the Mind*, edited by Brie Gertler and Lawrence Shapiro, Routledge, 2007.

Strawson, Peter. *Individuals*. Methuen & Co. Ltd, 1959.

Tulving, Endel. "Episodic Memory: From Mind to Brain." *Annual Review of Psychology*, vol. 53, no. 1, 2002.

Tulving, Endel, and Wayne Donaldson. *Organization of Memory*. Office of Naval Research, 1972.

Tumulty, Maura. "How Philosophers Think about Persons, Personal Identity, and the Self." *Personal Identity and Fractured Selves: Perspectives from Philosophy, Ethics, and Neuroscience*, edited by Deborah Mathews and J.H. Mathews, et al., John Hopkins UP, 2009, pp. 15–37.

Velleman, David. *Practical Reflection*. Princeton UP, 1989.

Vilariño, Idea. "Alms." Translated by Jesse Lee Kercheval. *The New Yorker*, Mar. 5, 2018.

Wellman, H.M. "Understanding the Psychological World: Developing a Theory of Mind." *Blackwell Handbook of Childhood Cognitive Development*, edited by U. Goswami, Blackwell Publishing, 2002, pp. 167–187.

White, Stephen L. *The Unity of the Self*. MIT Press, 1991.

Willard, Nancy. "'Who Invented Water?' Magic, Craft, and the Making of Children's Books." *Angel in the Parlor: Five Stories and Eight Essays*. Bookthrift Co., 1983.

Winnicott, W.D. *The Child the Family and the Outside World*. Penguin Press, 2000/1964.

Wittgenstein, Ludwig. *Philosophical Investigations*. Translated by G.E.M. Anscombe. Basil Blackwell Publisher Ltd., 1953.

Wollheim, Richard. *The Thread of Life*. Harvard UP, 1984.

Woolf, Virginia. *A Writer's Diary*. Hogarth Press, 1953.

Yeats, William Butler. "Per Amica Silentia Lunae." *A Routledge Literary Sourcebook on the Poems of W.B. Yeats*, edited by Michael O'Neill, Taylor & Francis, 2004/1918.

Young, Phillips E. "The Irony of Ironic Liberalism." *International Studies in Philosophy*, vol. 29, no. 1, 1997, pp. 121–130.

Zizek, Slavoj. *The Parallax View*. MIT Press, 2006.

———. *First as Tragedy, Then as Farce*. Verso, 2009.

Zuckert, Rachel. "Awe or Envy: Herder Contra Kant on the Sublime." *The Journal of Aesthetics and Art Criticism*, vol. 61, no. 3, 2003, pp. 217–232.

Index

190 **Why It's OK** to Be of Two Minds

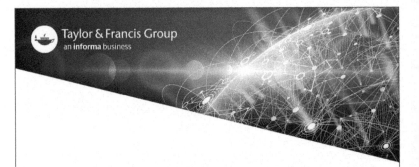

Milton Keynes UK
Ingram Content Group UK Ltd.
UKHW022340181023
430884UK00013B/96